Mke Nyumbani

Mke Nyumbani
Alice Taabu's Cookery Book

Kenway Publications
Nairobi • Kampala • Dar es Salaam

Published by Kenway Publications
a subsidiary of
East African Educational Publishers Ltd.
Brick Court, Mpaka Road/Woodvale Grove
Westlands, P.O. Box 45314
Nairobi

East African Educational Publishers Ltd.
P.O. Box 11542
Kampala

Ujuzi Educational Publishers Ltd.
P.O. Box 31647, Kijito-Nyama
Dar es Salaam

ISBN 9966-25-021-2

Typeset by Hi-Tech Typesetters Ltd., Nairobi

*Cover photo: Courtesy of the Communications Department,
Kenya Power and Lighting Company Ltd., Nairobi*

Printed in Kenya by Sunlitho Ltd.
P.O. Box 13939, Nairobi

TABLE OF CONTENTS

Dedication

To my beloved daughters, Rehema and Mbeyu.

PREFACE

This particular cookery book has been compiled as a result of the many requests. both verbal and written, from a multitude of viewers and cookery lovers of the extremely popular television programme initially titled "Mke Nyumbani" and now known as "Upishi Bora".

Having acquired on the job experience for more than 30 years with Kenya Power and Lighting Company Ltd., during which time I have been presenting the cookery programme for more than 20 years, I have shared this immensely satisfying experience with many of you through the popular cookery programme. I now wish to share that same experience with you through this cookery book.

As many of you will recall, I started presenting the "Mke Nyumbani" T.V. series in 1976 and have managed to cook with you over 500 simple, tested and affordable recipes.

Let us not forget that the pride of any family is in the well-being of its members, and that one way in which to achieve this is through being well fed with delicious and nutritious foods. It is, therefore, the responsibility of every cook to choose and prepare well-nourishing food. It is through a good diet that people are able to become more productive in their daily lives. There is a saying that goes, "A well fed society helps to build a strong nation".

Apart from cookery items in this book, there are also handy tips and hints to assist the reader in case of need.

It is, therefore, my sincere hope that this cookery book will serve to entertain and to teach all age-groups.

Alice Taabu
February, 2001

APPRECIATION

My appreciation goes to all of you who requested for and encouraged me to venture into writing this cookery book; to the editors and the publishers who were extremely patient and supportive; to the producers and crew of the Kenya Broadcasting Corporation, Mombasa station; to my colleagues; and, last but not least, to my family without whose patience and encouragement the writing of this book would not have become a reality.

My sincere thanks go to the members of the Board of Directors of Kenya Power and Lighting Company Ltd. for their faith in my ability to present the television programme 'Mke Nyumbani(now Upishi Bora)' under their sponsorship.

WEIGHTS, MEASURES AND SUBSTITUTES

These suggestions on weights, measures and substitutes are what are recommended by the author of this book and do not necessarily apply to all other cases.

Weights and Measures

Imperial	Cup	Metric Equivalent
1 oz		25g
4 oz	1c	100g
8 oz	2c	200g
1 lb	4c	400g
2 lb	8c	1kg

Liquids

1 fluid oz		25ml
5 fluid oz		125ml
$\frac{1}{2}$ pt		250g
1 pt		500g
$1\frac{3}{4}$ pt		1 lt

Substitutes

In this section, you have some substitutes that could come in handy in case you do not get the recommended ingredients.

Ingredients	Substitutes
1 cup yoghurt	– 1 cup of milk plus 1 Tblsp lemon or lime juice or vinegar.
1 cup honey or golden syrup	– Boil 1 cup of sugar and $\frac{1}{4}$ cup of water until the mixture is of honey consistency.
2 egg yolks	– 1 whole egg
1 tsp baking powder	– mix $\frac{1}{4}$ tsp of bicarbonate of soda and $\frac{1}{2}$ tsp of cream of tartar.
1 Tblsp flour for thickening	– $\frac{1}{2}$ tblsp of cornflour.
1 cup S.R.Flour	– 1 cup of plain flour plus $\frac{1}{2}$ tsp baking powder and a pinch of salt.
1 cup thin coconut milk	– 1 cup milk.
1 cup thick coconut milk	– $\frac{1}{2}$ cup of milk plus $\frac{1}{2}$ cup of cream.

Oven Temperature

Oven heat is very important to the success of any baking. Below is a guideline on different degrees of heat:

Ordinary heat	Fahrenheit degrees	Celcius degrees	Gas numbers
Very low	150-325	70-170	$\frac{1}{4}$-3
Moderate	325-400	170-200	3-6
Hot	400-475	200-240	6-9
Very Hot	475-500	240-290	9-10

ABBREVIATIONS

C	=	Cup
tblsp	=	Tablespoon
tsp	=	teaspoon
ml	=	mililitre
kg	=	Kilogram
g	=	Gram
flour	=	Plain white wheat flour
oz	=	Ounce
lb	=	Pound
lt	=	Litre
pt	=	Pint
L	=	Level
S.R. Flour	=	Self raising flour

COOKERY TERMS

The terms below appear often in this cookery book:

BASTE	-	To spoon hot liquid over meat whilst cooking.
BEAT	-	To beat briskly to lighten the mixture.
BLANCH	-	To place food in hot water for a short time.
BLEND	-	To mix ingredients, e.g., egg with milk.
BONE	-	To remove bones from meat or fish.
BOURQUET GARNISH	-	A bunch of selected herbs tied together. The commonly used ones are bay leaf, parsley, thyme or rosemary.
BRAISE	-	To cook meat in a rich brown sauce.
CHILL	-	To allow to become very cold but not frozen.
CHOP	-	Cut food in smaller pieces using a sharp knife.
COAT	-	Cover food with flour, eggs or bread crumbs.
CREAM	-	To stir, beat or rub with a spoon or electric beater until soft, smooth and creamy.
DECORATE	-	To add extra ingredients to make the dish look attractive, especially sweet dishes.
DICE	-	Cut food into small even pieces.
DILUTE	-	To reduce the thickness, sweetness or bitterness of food by adding more liquid.
DREDGE	-	Coat liberally with flour or sugar.
DUST	-	Coat lightly with flour or sugar.
FLAKE	-	To split food into smaller pieces with a fork or a knife.
FOLD	-	Movement used to mix flour in a cake mixture.
GARNISH	-	Same as decorate, but garnish is used on savoury dishes.
GLAZE	-	To give a shine on food by brushing with egg, milk or milk and sugar.
GRATE	-	To shred food with a grater.
GRILL	-	Cook under a hot grill or very hot charcoal .
KNEAD	-	Mix dough with hands on a board.

MASH	-	To pound food to make it smooth.
PARBOIL	-	Boil food in salted water for a short time and drain it before its cooked.
PARE/PEEL	-	To remove the outer skin of vegetable or fruit using a knife.
PIPE	-	To press a mixture through a shape pipe, e.g., cream or icing sugar or mashed potatoes, as in cake decoration.
POACH	-	Cook food slowly in water or milk as in poached eggs or fish.
PROVE	-	To put bread dough in a warm place to rise.
PUREE	-	Cook solid food until soft and pass it through a sieve or a blender.
ROAST	-	To cook by dry heat in an oven or over charcoal.
ROUX	-	A mixture of fat and flour to which liquid is added to make gravy or sauce.

DIFFERENT METHODS OF COOKING

1. **BOIL:** To cook food in a liquid at a boiling temperature. This method is misunderstood by many cooks, especially when cooking meat. Food cooks faster when simmered and not when boiled.

2. **BARBECUE:** To cook food with direct heat, either under a hot grill, over charcoal or in an oven, basting frequently with sauce or gravy.

3. **BRAISE:** To cook slowly in a small amount of liquid in a tight covered utensil on top of a cooker or in an oven. Usually the food is browned in a small amount of fat before braising. This method is used in pot roast.

4. **FRY:** To cook in hot fat or oil over dry heat. The word *Sauté* is also applied.

    a) Pan-fry: To brown foods slightly in a little gravy. Normally it is the first step in braising and gives the brown basis for most gravies.

    b) Shallow fat frying: To cook food in a medium amount of oil, about enough to cover half the food. The method is used for cooking fritters, etc.

    c) Deep frying: To cook food in a lot more oil, enough to cover the food. This method is used in cooking doughnuts, potato chips and batter coated foods.

5. **GRILL:** To cook food by exposing to direct heat, usually under a grill or over charcoal.

6. **POACH:** To cook food in a liquid at or below the simmering point taking precautions to retain the shape of food. This method is used in making eggs and fish.

7. **ROAST:** To cook by dry heat in an oven or over charcoals.

8. **STEAM:** To cook by steam in a closed container. The method is used in making dumplings and puddings. To steam-bake is to cook in an oven in a pan set over a container of hot water.

9. **STEW:** To simmer slowly in a small amount of liquid in a covered pan. Another word for stewing is fricassee.

10. **TOAST:** To brown by direct heat in a toaster, under a grill or over charcoal.

PART ONE

INTRODUCTION

- Useful Hints in Cookery
- Food Hygiene
- Making Use of Leftovers
- How to Avoid Accidents in the Kitchen

USEFUL HINTS IN COOKERY

When cooking, something could go wrong and you would need a solution.
Below are some hints on the problems you could encounter and suggestions on remedial measures:

Stews

Problem:

a)   If the stew is too salty

Remedy:

 1.   Peel a few potatoes and add to the boiling stew until they are cooked.

 2.   Remove the potatoes since they have absorbed the excess salt.

 3.   Remember to use less salt next time you cook.

b)   If the stew becomes too oily.

Remedy:

 1.   Keep it aside after cooking until it cools down and the oil settles then scoop out the oil with a spoon

 2.   Dip a clean cloth on the oil. The cloth will absorb the oil.

 3.   Place a slice of bread on the stew and it will absorb the oil. Remove the bread.

Placing bread on stew to absorb oil

 4.   Cover ice cubes with a clean cloth and dip them into the stew. The ice will freeze the oil which will then cling onto the cloth.

 5.   Pour the cold stew into a dish and place it in the fridge until the oil sets. Remove the oil with a spoon.

c)   If the stew becomes watery.

Remedy:

1. Mix a little cornflour with a little cold water into a paste and stir into the stew.
2. Mix a little plain flour with a little margarine. Pour it into the stew and stir.
3. Mix a little gravy thickening with cold water and stir into the stew.

Fish

Problem:

If the Fish breaks into pieces while being fried.

Remedy:

1. The fish may have gone bad. Discard it immediately as it will emit a bad smell and attract flies.
2. The fish may be undercooked; try cooking it longer.
3. Sprinkle flour on the fish before cooking.

Sprinkling flour on fish before cooking

Meat

Problem:

If cooked meat is too tough.

Remedy:

Different cuts of meat require different types of cooking, i.e., boiling, stewing, frying and roasting. Apply the right method of cooking to the different cuts.

If liver becomes too hard.

Remedy:

1. It means it was overcooked. Try coating liver with flour after removing the veins and skin. The flour will stop the juices from drying.
2. Cook for a shorter time.

4

Vegetables

Problem:

If vegetables are tasteless after cooking.

Remedy:

1. It means they were cut into big pieces and overcooked in too much water. You may improve the flavour by adding a little butter or peanut butter
2. Cut vegetables into small pieces to enable them cook within a short time.
3. Cook vegetables in very little water or fat.

Pickles and Jams

Problem:

a) If pickles and jam form a mould in the bottle, the reasons are:
   i) They were kept in a warm place.
   ii) The bottles used for storage were not the right type. For example, plastic instead of glass.
   iii) The preservation ingredient was not enough.
   iv) The fruits used were too ripe.

Remedy:

1. For jam, remove the mould, cook it again and use it at once.
2. For pickles or other sour fruits, discard them immediately as they can be poisonous

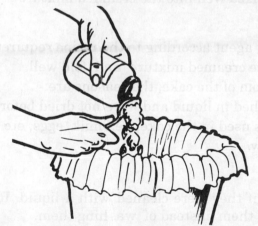

Discarding of moulded fruit

Jelly

Problem:

a) If Jelly fails to set, the reasons are likely to be:
   i) Too much liquid was used.
   ii) The gelatine was not enough.
   iii) The jelly was placed in a warm place to set.
   iv) Fresh pineapples were used in the recipe.

Remedy:

    i)   Reduce the amount of liquid.

    ii) Increase the quantity of gelatine.

    iii) Place it in the refrigerator in order for it to set properly, but not in the freezer compartment.

Cakes

Cakes prepared by the creaming method

Problem:

a)   If cakes are soggy, the reasons are:

    i)   The cake mixture was beaten for too long.

    ii) Too much S.R. flour was used.

    iii) It was not baked at the right temperature. The heat was too low.

    iv) The cake was left to cool in the baking tin.

Remedy:

    i)   After creaming the sugar and fat, beat the eggs for only a few seconds. In case the mixture shows signs of curdling, add a little flour. Fold the flour very gently but fast.

    ii) Bake at the right temperature.

    iii) Turn out the cake onto a cooling wire rack to cool.

b)   If a cake develops many holes, the reasons are likely to be:

    i)   Too much raising agent was used.

    ii) The flour was not mixed well into the creamed mixture

Remedy:

    i)   Measure the raising agent according to the recipe requirement.

    ii) Sift the flour into the creamed mixture and fold well.

c)   If fruits sink to the bottom of the cake, the reasons are:-

    i)   The fruits were washed in liquid and were not dried before being used.

    ii) Too much liquid was used in the cake, i.e., milk, eggs, etc.

    iii) The heat was too low.

Remedy:

    i)   Dry the fruits well if they were cleaned with a liquid. Rub fruits with flour and then sieve them instead of washing them.

    ii) The mixture should not be too soft.

    iii) Bake at the right temperature.

d)   If the cake crack on top, the reasons are:

    i)   The oven was hotter than required.

    ii) Too much flour was used.

    iii) The mixture was too thick.

Remedy:

    i)   Bake at the right temperature.
    ii) Measure the flour correctly.
    iii) Add in enough liquid to give the correct consistency.

e)   If the cake sinks in the centre, the reasons are:-

    i)   The mixture was too soft.
    ii) The fat content was too high.
    iii) Too much heat was used in baking.
    iv) The cake was shaken whilst being baked.
    v)   The oven door was opened whilst baking, thus allowing in cold air and dropping the oven temperature.

Remedy:

    i)   Test the texture before baking.
    ii) Measure the fat correctly.
    iii) Bake at the recommended temperature.
    iv) Avoid knocking against the cooker while baking.
    v)   Do not open the oven door until the cake has had at least three quarters of its baking time in the oven.

Cakes prepared by the whisking method:

Problem:

a)   If cakes are soggy, the reasons are:

    i)   The eggs and sugar mixture was not whisked to the correct consistency.
    ii) Too much flour was used.
    iii) The oven temperature was too low.
    iv) The cake was cooled in the baking tin.

Remedy:

    i)   Whisk the eggs and sugar until the mixture is thick enough to leave a trail when lifted.
    ii) Use the recommended amount of flour.
    iii) Bake at the right temperature.
    iv) Cool the cake on a wire rack immediately it is removed from the oven.

b)   If the cake becomes heavy and sinks in the centre, the reasons are:

    i)   The cake was removed from the oven before it was ready.
    ii) The oven was too hot and, therefore, the cake browned without being cooked.

7

Remedy:

    i)   Bake the cake until ready. To determine if it is properly cooked, pierce it with a clean skewer or a knitting needle. The needle or skewer should come out clean if the cake is cooked.

    ii)   Bake at the right temperature.

c)   If the cake is cooked but the centre is raised and cracked, the reasons are:

    i)   The mixture was beaten for too long.

    ii)   Too much raising agent was used.

Remedy:

    i)   Beat the mixture just long enough to mix the flour well.

    ii)   Use the recommended amount of raising agent.

    iii) Slice off the raised portion to make the cake even. Turn it upside down and decorate.

d)   If the cake is too brown and dry around the edges, the reasons are:-

    i)   Too much heat was used.

    ii)   The cake was baked for too long.

    iii) The cake was baked from the bottom shelve of a gas oven.

    iv) The cake was baked from the top shelf of an electric or charcoal oven.

Remedy:

    i)   Bake from the right shelf.

    ii)   Bake at right temperatures.

    iii) Observe recommended baking time.

The cake can be made edible by doing the following:

i)   Scrap off the over-browned edges and burnt sides with a sharp knife.

ii)   If too dry, try sprinkling the cake with fruit juice or wine to moisten it a little.

Left Over Cakes

A left over cake that has dried or lost some of its flavour can be used in the following way:

i)   It can be reheated in an oven and made soft again.

ii)   A fruit cake can be sliced and fried in a little butter to improve the flavour.

iii) It can be crushed into crumbs and used to make a pudding.

Rice

Rice or pasta has become soggy after cooking for the following reasons:-

Problem:

i)   Cooking in too much water.

ii)   Cooking for too long.

iii) Going cold in the water it was cooked in.

Remedy:
i)   Cook in the recommended amount of water.
ii)   Cook for the recommended period of time and add a little oil or butter.
iii) Flush the rice or pasta in cold water immediately after cooking and reheat it.

Pastries

Problem:

a)   Pastry can lose its shape and become hard for the following reasons:
    i)   It was handled too much.
    ii)   Too much liquid was used in making pastry.
    iii) Too little heat was used for baking the pastry.
    iv)   Pastry was overstretched during rolling.

Remedy:
    i)   Handle the pastry as little as possible.
    ii)   Do not exceed the recommended liquid.
    iii) Bake in sufficient heat.
    iv)   Do not overstretch the pastry when rolling.

Problem:

b)   If pastry breaks unnecessarily before or after cooking, the reasons are:
    i)   Too much fat was used.
    ii)   Too little liquid was used.
    iii) Too much handling and kneading of pastry.

Remedy:
i)   Use less fat.
ii)   If it is too hard, try adding a little water, egg or milk.
iii) Lift the pastry with a knife instead of using your fingers.

Biscuits

Problem:

If biscuits become too soft after baking, the reasons are likely to be:
i)   The biscuits were not baked for long enough.
ii)   The tin used to store the biscuit does not close well and allows in moisture.

Remedy:
i)   Return the biscuits onto the baking tray and bake them in a hot oven for a few minutes. Remove the baking tray from the oven and transfer the biscuits onto a wire rack after about 10 minutes.
ii)   Store in an airtight tin.
iii) Line the tin with sheets of grease proof paper and arrange the biscuits in a layer before closing it tightly.

9

Bread

a)   If the dough does not rise properly, the reasons are:

Problem:

   i)   The quantity of yeast used is too low.
   ii)   The yeast is not active.
   iii) The liquid used to reconstitute the yeast was either too hot or too cold
   iv)   The dough was not covered and kept in a warm place to rise.

Remedy:

   i)   Use the correct quantity of yeast.
   ii)   To find out if the yeast is active, sprinkle a little warm water into the cup with the yeast and place it in a warm place. Bubbles should appear on the surface.
   iii) The liquid should be luke warm.
   iv)   Keep the covered dough in a warm place until it rises.

Problem:

b)   If bread smells of yeast, the reasons are:
   i)   Too much yeast was used.
   ii)   The dough was left to rise for a longer time than necessary.

Remedy:

i)   Use the correct quantity of yeast.
ii)   Dough should rise to about double its original size.

Problem:

c)   If bread rises higher on one side of the tin than the other, the reasons are:
   i)   The dough was not spread evenly in the tin
   ii)   The dough was not kneaded well enough to allow the even distribution of air.

Remedy:

i)   Press the dough evenly into the tin using the back of your fingers.
ii)   Knead the dough thoroughly. To check if the air is well distributed, cut through the dough with a sharp knife. There should be only very small well scattered holes in the dough. Large holes are a sign of air that is not well distributed.

FOOD HYGIENE

Food prepared under dirty conditions can be dangerous. Preparations and cooking of food must, therefore, be done in a clean environment. It is also important to note that visible dirt is even more dangerous because it harbours bacteria which can easily cause food poisoning.

10

Bacteria are minute living organisms found everywhere, including the air, water, soil, our bodies and the food we cook.

It is important to observe the following rules:

1. Rules on Food Hygiene

a) Food must not be touched with hands that have been in contact with any dirty surfaces.

b) Food must be protected from flies, mice and domestic animals.

c) Food must be prepared, cooked, served and stored in clean utensils and handled with clean tools.

d) Food must be cooked when fresh.

e) Cold food should be stored in a cool place.

f) Should there be a need to store food for a longer time, a refrigerator is necessary.

2. Personal Cleanliness of the Food Handler or Cook:

a) Hands must be washed with soap and wiped dry before handling food, especially after visiting the toilet or using a handkerchief.

b) Nails should be kept short and clean.

c) Never scratch yourself, lick your fingers or poke them into the mouth, nose, ears or any other part of the body while preparing food.

d) Cuts and sores must be covered with waterproof elastoplast.

e) Avoid preparing or cooking food when suffering from an infectious disease.

f) Avoid handling of food with hands as much as possible. Use proper equipment like tongs, forks and spoons.

3. Cleanliness in the Kitchen:

a) The kitchen must be kept spotlessly clean.

b) There should be nothing to attract flies, mice or beetles.

c) Food spilt on the floor or cupboards must be swept or wiped away at once.

d) Cooking utensils must be cleaned with soap, rinsed and dried with clean tea clothes before storage.

e) All kitchen clothes should be washed daily, boiled at least twice a week and ironed.

f) Working surfaces must be cleaned daily.

g) The floor should be swept and washed daily.

h) Arrange the food store regularly.

General comment

Make sure that food is free from infection or contamination by maintaining high standards of cleanliness of the kitchen and the food handler.

MAKING USE OF LEFTOVERS

Leftover food should not be looked down upon when planning a menu. They can be made into very delicious dishes.

1. Left over stew or curry can be made into a casserole or pie. Cook and mash potatoes, add a little milk and spread over the left over stew in a casserole. Brush the top with egg and bake.

2. Different kinds of meat from leftover roast can be minced and made into pasties or pinwheel with short crust pastry.

3. Pieces of chicken or ham can be shredded and added to an omelette or scrambled eggs or added to a green salad.

4. Leftover cooked vegetables can be made into casseroles and sprinkled with cheese.

5. Raw leftover vegetables can be turned into delicious soups and stuffing for chicken or meat.

6. Leftover fruit salads can be stewed with a little sugar and consumed or made into jam by adding more sugar. They can also be used as a filling for a cake.

7. Leftover bread and cakes can be made into bread and butter puddings or triffles. They can also be dried and crushed into bread crumbs.

HOW TO AVOID ACCIDENTS IN THE KITCHEN

Some of us live in towns where electricity is the main source of energy. Electricity can make work easy and enjoyable but if used carelessly, it can be very dangerous.

Below are a few tips on how to reduce accidents emanating from the usage of this vital energy, and others that occur at home:

1. Ensure the plug tops fitted on electrical appliances, e.g., electric iron, kettle, food mixers, etc., are dry before plugging into socket outlets. This will prevent any risk of electric shock or electric fires.

2. Make a habit of checking all plugs and switches for any loose fittings or thread bare insulated flexes. The exposed wires on flex may be dangerous if touched with naked or wet hands when the appliances are switched on.

3. Avoid fitting a long flex on an electrical appliance because it may cause someone to trip over, or a child may pull at it. One should be able to monitor it at close range from a power point to the electrical appliance in use.

4. All electrical appliances should be supervised when being utilised and must be switched off immediately after use. Electrical appliances like irons, cookers, kettles etc., left unattended can cause fires.

5. Do not let electrical appliance flexes hang into the sink or wet surface because they may get soaked in water and cause an electric shock.

6. Switch off an electric kettle and unplug it from the socket before filling it or pouring water from it. Remember to fill a kettle with enough water to cover the heating element. If elements are heated dry, they will burn and spoil the Kettle.

7. Socket covers should be used to cover sockets in homes with children.

8. All plugs must be wired and fused correctly.

9. If bread gets stuck in the toaster while toasting, switch off the toaster and unplug it. Allow it to cool then remove the bread by shaking the toaster while upside down. Avoid pocking metal implement into the heating element when the toaster is on.

10. Do not switch on any electric appliance with wet hands.

11. Repair faulty electrical appliances immediately you detect the fault. They can be the cause of power wastage and may also lead to electric shock or fires.

Other accidents

12. Safeguard against leaving handles of saucepans and frying pans containing hot food projecting over the edge of a cooker or kitchen table. An inquisitive child may want to find out its contents, thereby tipping the pan over its upturned face and consequently getting burnt. Turn all the pan handles inwards .

13. Hot oil should never be left unattended, especially when deep frying. Fry a little food at a time and only when young children are not close by. Oil must never be more than half a pan full as it may boil over and ignite upon contact with the fire.

14. Be extra careful when using pressure cookers. The lid should be removed only after the pressure in the cooker has escaped. It should never be forced off. Remember to read all the instructions on the appliance before use.

15. During cooking, avoid long sleeved and very loose garments as they can easily get in contact with fire.

16. A sharp knife used with care on a chopping board is safer than a blunt knife. Use all sharp objects in the kitchen with greater caution.

17. Never leave children alone with fire or with anything that can ignite a fire.

18. Should hot oil catch fire, do not open doors and windows since draught will make matters worse. Switch off the cooker immediately and cover the pan containing the oil with a lid or a wet sack. Sand can be used to extinguish the flames.

19. If someone catches fire, close all air vents and try to put it off by rolling a heavy blanket or heavy coat around the burning person. Send or call for medical attention at once.

20. When uncovering pans with hot food, move the lids away from you. The same procedure applies to opening hot oven doors and grills.

21. Use a heavy dry tea cloth or oven gloves to lift hot pans, tins or casseroles from the cooker. Wet light kitchen clothes can easily heat up and slip from your hands.

22. Use a firm ladder or chair to reach high stored items. Store frequently used items on lower shelves, less used items on upper shelves and the heavy items within easy reach.

23. Avoid table clothes that hang low and keep hot food and drinks away from the table edges. A crawling child may be tempted to pull down the hanging table cloth.

PART TWO

RECIPES

- Biscuits and Snacks
- Bread
- Cakes
- Chicken
- Fish
- Fruit Dishes
- Meat
- Puddings
- Vegetable Dishes
- Other Dishes

Biscuits and Snacks

Cardamon Biscuits

Pastry Cases

Puff Pastry

Pan Scones

Orange Maizemeal Biscuits

Nut Crescents

Mahamri (Yeast)

Mandazi (Baking Powder)

Lemon Drop Doughnuts

Lemon Cookies

Gram Flour Bhajias

Drop Scones

Digestive Biscuits

Cream Horns

Cornish Pasties

Coconut Rings

Chocolate Biscuits

Cheese Straws

Cheese Scones

Cheese Puffs

Carrot Biscuits

Cardamon Biscuit

5 oz flour

$\frac{1}{2}$ tsp ground cardamons

2 tblsp sugar

2 oz margarine

3 tblsp golden syrup or honey

Method:

Sift the flour with cardamon and mix with sugar. Melt the margarine and stir in the syrup. Stir in the dry ingredients and mix well. Form into small balls and place on baking trays. Flatten with a fork. Bake at 350°F for 15 to 20 minutes. Cool slightly before removing from the tray.

Pastry cases

Pastry
- 8 oz flour
- Salt
- 4 oz margarine
- Water to mix
- Seasoning

Filling
- 2 hard boiled eggs
- 1 cup grated carrots
- $\frac{1}{2}$ cup cooked peas
- $\frac{1}{2}$ cup mayonnaise

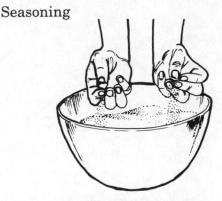

Rubbing fat into flour

Using a round cutter

Method:

Sift the flour with salt and rub in the fat. Add enough water to bind the mixture. Knead and roll out to $\frac{1}{4}$ inch thickness. Cut with a large round cutter and line the pastry tins with it. Bake blind at 350°F for 15 minutes. Remove the paper with rice and continue cooking the cases for five more minutes. Cool and fill.

Filling:

Chop the eggs and mix them with the rest of the ingredients. Fill the mixture into the cooled cases. Serve immediately.

Note: To bake blind is to fill the unbaked pastry shell with pieces of grease proof paper and fill each with raw rice.

Puff Pastry

400 g flour

400 g Margarine

1 oz lemon juice

7 oz ice cold water

Method:

Sift the flour and rub in 75g of the margarine. Bind with water and lemon juice. Roll out into an oblong and place a slab of the remaining margarine on it. Fold the pastry and roll it. Fold into three and let them chill for 30 minutes. Roll and fold twice more. Use as required.

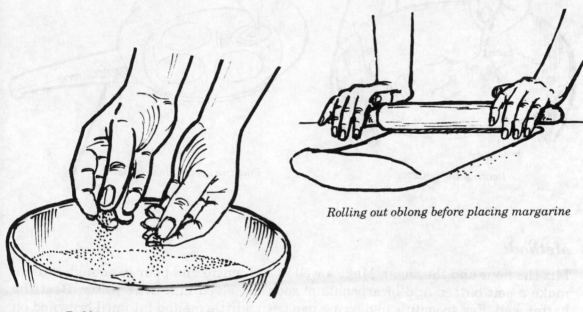

Rolling out oblong before placing margarine

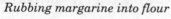

Rubbing margarine into flour

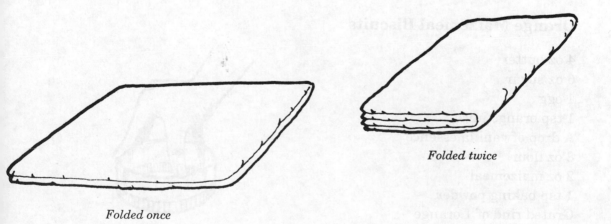

Folded twice

Folded once

Pan Scones

200 g flour

Sour milk

25 g sugar

1 tsp bicarbonate of soda

A little fat

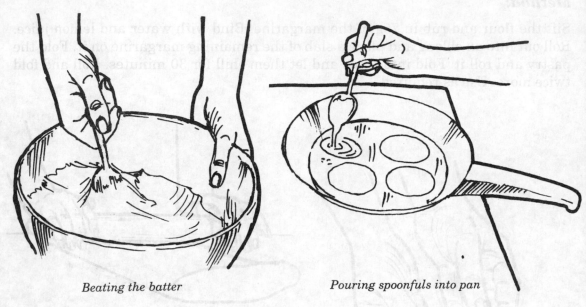

Beating the batter   *Pouring spoonfuls into pan*

Method:

Mix the flour and the sugar. Make a well in the centre and pour in enough milk to make a soft batter. Add bicarbonate of soda dissolved in a little water. Beat the batter well. Fry spoonfuls in a frying pan with a little melted fat until browned on both sides. Serve with butter and jam.

Orange Maizemeal Biscuits

4 oz butter

6 oz sugar

1 egg

1 tsp orange juice

A drop of vanilla essence

8 oz flour

2 oz maizemeal

1 tsp baking powder

Grated rind of 1 orange

Orange glace icing

Using fluted cutters

Method:

Cream the butter and the sugar. Beat in the egg, orange juice and vanilla. Sift in the dry ingredients. Knead in the rind. Roll out and cut with flutted cutters. Place on a greased tray. Bake at 375°F for 12 to 15 minutes. When cool, top with orange icing.

Nut Cresents

1 cup margarine	2 cups flour
$\frac{1}{2}$ cup sugar	1 tsp baking powder
2 egg yolks	1 cup chopped walnuts or cashewnuts
1 tsp flavouring	

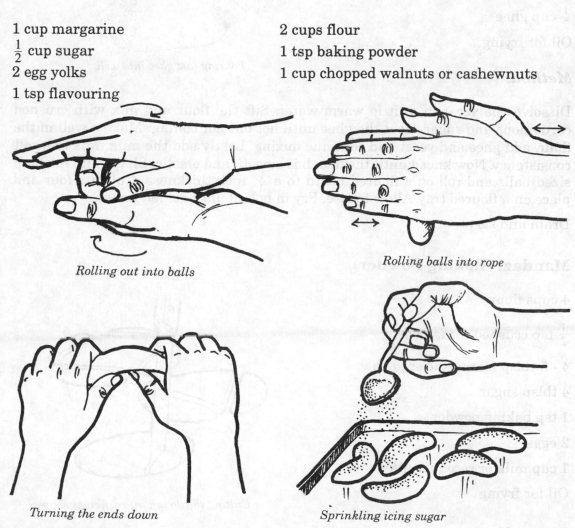

Rolling out into balls

Rolling balls into rope

Turning the ends down

Sprinkling icing sugar

Method:

Mix well the margarine, sugar, yolks and flavouring. Sift in the flour and baking powder. Add the nuts and knead well. Cut into small balls and roll on a floured board or with hands into a long rope — about 2" long. Turn the ends down and shape into a crescent. Place on a greased baking tray and bake at 350°F for 10 to 12 minutes. Cool and dust with icing sugar.

Mahamri (Yeast)

4 cups flour

4 tblsp sugar

A few cardamons (5-10)

1 tsp yeast

$\frac{3}{4}$ cup warm water

2 cups milk or coconut milk

$\frac{1}{2}$ cup ghee

Oil for frying

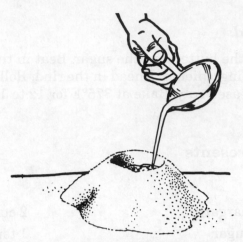

Pouring last ghee into well

Method:

Dissolve the yeast in a little warm water. Sift the flour and mix with crushed cardamons and sugar. Heat the ghee until hot but not boiling. Make a well in the flour, add ghee and yeast and continue mixing. Lastly add the milk. Mix to a soft consistency. Now knead until the dough is smooth and elastic. Shape into medium sized balls and roll on a floured board to a $\frac{1}{4}$ inch thickness. Cut into four and place on a floured tray. Allow to rise. Fry in hot oil until golden brown.

Drain and serve.

Mandazi (Baking Powder)

4 cups flour

$\frac{1}{2}$ tsp crushed cardamons

4 - 5 tblsp margarine or ghee

4 tblsp sugar

1 tsp baking powder

2 eggs

1 cup milk or coconut milk

Oil for frying

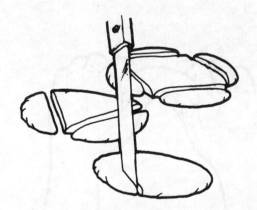

Cutting the dough into different shapes

Method:

Sift the flour and the other dry ingredients together. Melt the fat and mix into the flour. Beat the eggs with a little milk and add to the flour. Add in more milk to make a soft dough and knead. Cut into small balls and roll out to about a $\frac{1}{4}$ inch thickness. Cut into different shapes. Heat the oil and fry until brown. Drain and serve.

Lemon Drop Doughnuts

1 egg

½ lemon juice

½ tablespoon lemon rind

2 oz sugar

1 tablespoon oil

4 oz flour

1 heaped teaspoon baking powder

1 teaspoon milk

Oil for frying

Finished doughnuts

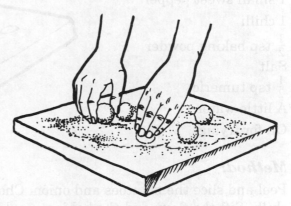

Tossing in sugar and cinnamon

Method:

Mix the egg, lemon juice, rind, sugar and oil in a bowl. Sift in the flour and the baking powder. Mix the flour, the milk and the rest of ingredients. Drop teaspoonfuls of the mixture into hot oil and fry until golden brown. Drain and toss into sugar and cinnamon.

Lemon Cookies

½ cup flour

½ tsp baking powder

½ cup butter

¾ cup sugar

1 egg

2 tsp lemon rind

1 Tblsp lemon juice

Flattening balls of dough

Dipping into sugar

Method:

Sift the dry ingredients. Cream, butter and sugar, add the egg and mix well. Add the remaining ingredients and knead into a dough. Chill for 15 minutes. Shape into balls, flatten and dip into the sugar. Bake at 350°F for 10 to 15 minutes.

Gram Flour Bhajias

$\frac{1}{4}$ kg gram flour

3 potatoes

1 onion

1 cup spinach

1 tblsp dania

1 small sweet pepper

1 chilli

$\frac{1}{2}$ tsp baking powder

Salt

$\frac{1}{2}$ tsp tumeric

A little water

Oil for frying

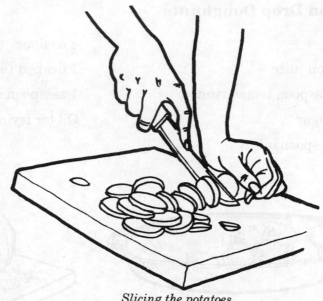

Slicing the potatoes

Method:

Peel and slice the potatoes and onion. Chop the spinach, sweet pepper, dania and chilli. Sift the flour and the baking powder into a bowl and add the salt, tumeric and enough water to form a soft but not dropping batter. Add all the vegetables and mix well. Heat the oil and fry small quantities of the mixture at a time until brown and cooked. Drain and serve with chutney.

Drop Scones

250g wheat flour

1 heaped tsp baking powder

A pinch of salt

25g sugar

1 egg

250mls milk

2 tblsp oil

Honey for serving

Beating the batter

Turning the drop scones

Method:

Sift the flour and baking powder into a bowl. Add the salt, sugar, egg and milk. Beat to form a smooth batter. Heat the oil and fry spoonfuls until bubbles appear on top of them. Turn and cook the underside. Serve with honey.

Digestive Biscuits

6 oz wholemeal flour

1 oz maizemeal

A pinch of salt

l tsp baking powder

3 oz margarine

3 tblsp milk

1 $\frac{1}{2}$ oz sugar

Method:

Mix the flour with maizemeal, salt and baking powder. Rub in the fat and stir in the sugar. Pour in the milk and knead into a soft dough. Roll it out very thinly, prick with a fork and cut it with a 2" cutter. Place on greased trays and bake at 375°F for 15 to 20 minutes. Cool and serve.

Cream Horns

1 lb puff pastry

1 beaten egg

Cold water

2 tblsp jam

Whipped cream

Chopped nuts

Method:

Roll the pastry and cut into 1" wide by 3" long strips. Grease the corn moulds and wind them with the pastry strips, overlapping the pastry. Moisten the overlapping edges with a little water. Trim off the excess pastry. Place the moulds on a floured sheet. Brush with beaten egg. Bake at 400°F for 15 minutes. Remove the moulds carefully before the pastry cools. Cool and fill with a mixture of cream and jam. Decorate with nuts.

Cornish Pastries

$\frac{1}{2}$ kg short crust pastry

$\frac{1}{2}$ kg steak

2 potatoes

2 onions

Salt, pepper

2 tblsp water

A little egg to glaze with

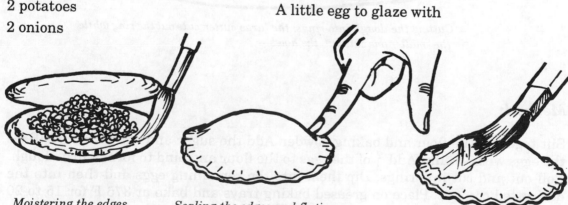

Moistering the edges using a brush

Sealing the edges and fluting

Brushing the top with egg

Method:

Make the pastry. Roll and cut into round shapes. Chop the meat. Peel the potatoes and onions and cut them into cubes. Put the meat, onions and potatoes into a plate and season well. Place them in the centre of the pastry and add the water. Brush the sides of the filled pastry with a little water and cover with the other round shaped pastry. Seal the edges together and flute. Place on greased baking trays. Brush the top with eggs and bake at 425°F for 25 minutes. Lower the heat to 350°F and bake for a further 25 minutes.

Coconut Rings

$\frac{1}{2}$ lb flour

1 tsp baking powder

$\frac{1}{4}$ lb butter

2 eggs

$\frac{1}{2}$ tsp vanilla essence

Desiccated coconut

$\frac{1}{2}$ cup sugar

Cutting the dough into rings: the large cutter cuts out the ring while the smaller one cuts out the holes

Method:

Sift together the flour and baking powder. Add the sugar and rub in the fat. Beat the eggs with vanilla. Add $\frac{2}{3}$ of the eggs to the flour and bind to form a firm dough. Roll out and cut into rings. Dip them into the remaining eggs and then into the desicatted coconut. Place on greased baking trays and bake at 375 F for 15 to 20 minutes.

26

Chocolate Biscuits

4 oz butter

2 oz sugar

1 tsp vanilla essence

4 oz self-raising flour

1 tablespoon cocoa

Pinch of salt

Method:

Cream the butter, sugar and vanilla to make them light. Fold in the cocoa, salt and sieved flour. Shape into small balls and place them on baking trays. Press them with a fork and bake at 400°F for 12 minutes.

Cheese Straws

8 oz flour

1 tsp baking powder

Salt, cayenne pepper

4 oz margarine

1 egg

4 oz cheese, grated

$\frac{1}{2}$ c Water

Method:

Sift together the flour, baking powder, salt and pepper and rub in the fat. Add the cheese and bind with the egg and water. Knead lightly and roll on a floured board. Cut into $\frac{1}{4}$" wide straws. Gather the remaining dough, roll and cut into rings with, first, a 3" cutter and then a 2" cutter. Place on baking trays and bake at 425°F for 7 to 10 minutes, or until brown. Cool and serve the straws in the rings.

Cheese Scones

200g flour

3 level tsp baking powder

$\frac{1}{4}$ tsp salt

50g margarine

100g grated cheese

Egg and milk

Method:

Sift together the flour, baking powder and salt. Rub in the fat and add the cheese. Gradually stir in the milk to make a soft dough. Turn onto a floured board and knead slightly. Roll to $\frac{3}{4}$ thickness. Cut into round scones, place on baking trays and brush the tops with a beaten egg and milk. Bake at 425°F for 7 to 10 minutes, or until golden brown.

Cheese Puffs

Filling:
- Salt pepper
- 4 oz cream cheese
- A little milk or cream

Choux Pastry:
- 3 oz flour
- $\frac{1}{4}$ pt water
- Pinch of sugar
- 1 oz margarine
- 2-3 small eggs

Method:

Place water, margarine and sugar in a pan and bring to boil. Add the flour and cook until dry and forms a ball. Remove the pan from the fire and add the eggs, one at a time, beating as you do so. Put the mixture into a piping bag and pipe onto greased trays. Bake at 425°F for 30 to 35 minutes. Cool and fill with cream cheese mixed with a little cream or milk.

Carrot Biscuits

- 8 oz margarine
- 8 oz flour
- 4 oz sugar
- $\frac{1}{2}$ tsp cinnamon
- $\frac{1}{4}$ tsp nutmeg
- 1 tsp vanilla
- 1 egg
- 6 oz grated carrots
- 2 oz nuts, chopped
- Extra Sugar

Cutting the rolls into slices

Method:

Cream the margarine until fluffy. Sift in the flour and mix with sugar and spices. Add the margarine, essence, egg, carrots and nuts and mix well. Shape into rolls, wrap with grease-proof paper and chill for at least two hours. Slice into pieces of $\frac{1}{2}$ inch thickness and bake at 375°F for 10 to 12 minutes. Sprinkle with sugar whilst warm.

Bread

Types of Bread

Bean Bread

Chapati

Coconut Bread

Crown Bread

Bread dough

Fruit and Nut Twist

Honey Loaf

Orange Oat Bread

Poppy Buns

Snow Ball Buns

Walnut, Fruit Loaf

Yeast Buns

Mabumbunda (Banana Bread)

Bean Bread

1 cup bean flour

2 cups wheat flour

2 tblsp margarine

A pinch of salt

2 tsp baking powder

1 or $1\frac{1}{2}$ cups of milk

Method:

Sift the two types of flours together with salt and baking powder. Rub in the margarine until the mixture looks like breadcrumbs. Bind the mixture with milk. Knead for a while. Place the shaped dough into a greased baking tin and bake at 375°F for about one hour.

Cool and serve.

Chapati

2 c flour

$\frac{1}{2}$ tsp salt

$\frac{1}{4}$ c oil

About 1c water

Oil for frying

Rubbing fat into flour

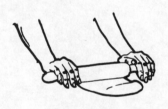

Rolling out the balls

Spreading fat on rolled-out ball

Folding before keeping aside

Method:

Sift the flour and salt. Rub in the fat and bind with water. Shape into medium sized balls. Roll out each ball and spread on more fat. Fold and keep aside. Roll out thinly and dry both sides on a hot pan. Apply a little oil and cook both sides until well browned.

Coconut Bread

100g margarine

100g sugar

2 eggs

150g S.R. flour

4 tblsp desiccated coconut

2 tblsp milk

Method:

Cream margarine and sugar until well blended. Beat in the eggs and, lastly, fold in the sifted flour with 3 tblsp of desiccated coconut and milk. Pour into a greased loaf tin and sprinkle the remaining desiccated coconut on it. Bake at 350°F for 1 to $1\frac{1}{4}$ hours, or until cooked and browned. Cool and serve.

Crown Bread

Bread dough

A little water

$\frac{1}{2}$ egg

A few poppy seeds

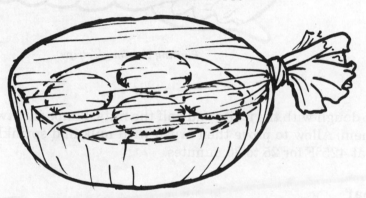

Rolls in polythene covered tin

Method:

Divide the dough into six and shape into balls. Place them in a greased 8" sandwich tin, five around the tin and one in the centre. Keep them in a slightly greased polythene bag until well risen (about 15 minutes). Brush with the egg mixed with water. Sprinkle with a few poppy seeds. Bake for 15 to 20 minutes at 450°F, or until cooked and well browned.

Bread Dough

$\frac{1}{2}$ kg flour

1 tsp yeast

1 tsp sugar

50g margarine

250ml milk, warm

1 beaten egg

Method:

Sift the flour into a bowl. Dissolve the yeast in a little warm milk and stir in the sugar. Warm the margarine and mix with the remaining milk. Make a well in the centre of the flour and put in the egg, yeast and warm milk. Mix to form a soft dough. Knead on a floured board until the dough is soft and pliable.

Fruit and Nut Twist

Bread dough
75g Sultanas

200g chopped nuts
A little milk for glazing

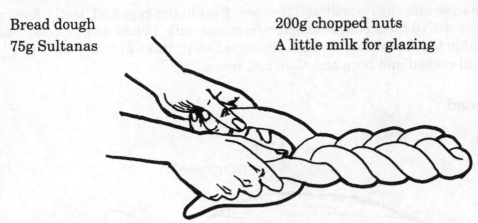

Plaiting the dough strips

Method:

Prepare the dough with the fruits and half the nuts. Shape into two or three strips and plait them. Allow to prove then brush with milk and sprinkle the remaining nuts. Bake at 425°F for 25 to 30 minutes.

Honey Loaf

175g S.R. flour
125g butter
100g brown sugar
150ml honey
1 tblsp water
2 eggs
Flaked almonds

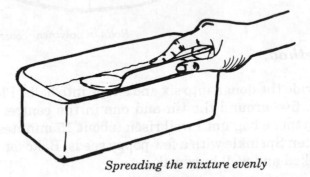

Spreading the mixture evenly

Method:

Place a pan with butter, sugar, honey and water on a low heat and stir occassionally until the butter melts. Draw off the heat and cool. Beat in the eggs, add the sifted flour and beat to a smooth mixture. Pour into a greased and lined tin of 11 x 7 inches in size. Spread out the mixture evenly and sprinkle with flaked almond. Place in the centre of an oven set at 350°F for 30 to 35 minutes, or until cooked. Cool and cut into slices.

Orange Oat Bread

1 tsp yeast
25g sugar
50g margarine
1 tsp golden syrup
75g oats

1 tsp grated orange rind
200g flour
125ml orange juice
hot water

Method:

Dissolve the yeast in warm water with 1 tsp Sugar. Mix the margarine, syrup, sugar, oats and rind in a bowl. Add the hot water, juice, the yeast mixture and flour and mix to a soft dough. Knead gently on a floured board until smooth. Place in a greased bowl. Cover and allow to rise to double its bulk. Shape into a loaf and place in a greased loaf tin. Let it rise again. Brush the top with water, sprinkle with a few oats and bake at 425°F for 15 minutes. Reduce the heat to 375°F and bake for another 30 minutes. Cool and serve.

Poppy Buns

400g flour
50g sugar
1 tsp yeast
2 tblsp warm water
50g margarine

250ml milk
1 egg
1 tsp honey or syrup
Poppy seeds

Method:

Sift the flour into a bowl. Heat the milk and margarine and let it cool to luke warm. Dissolve the yeast in a little warm water. Make a well in the centre of the flour and pour in the yeast, sugar and egg. Mix with the milk, a little at a time, until a soft dough forms. Knead until smooth. Place into a greased bowl, cover and allow to rise to double its size. Knead again, shape into buns and place on a greased baking tray. Allow to rise again, brush with honey and sprinkle with poppy seeds. Bake at 425°F for 20 minutes.

Snow Ball Buns

150g self raising flour
50g margarine
50g sugar
1 egg
A few drops of Vanilla essence

A little water
3 tblsp apricot jam
25g desiccated coconut
Cherries and angelica

Decorated rolls in cups

Method:

Sift the flour and rub in the margarine. Add the sugar and bind with egg, water and vanilla essence. Knead lightly and divide into 20 equal pieces. Roll up each piece into a ball and place on a greased baking tray. Bake at 400°F. for 7 to 10 minutes, or until golden brown. When cold, brush them with sieved and warmed jam. Roll them into the coconut and decorate with cherries and angelica. Serve in paper cake cases.

Walnut Fruit Loaf

100g margarine

100g sugar

2 eggs

$\frac{1}{4}$ pt milk

300g mixed fruit

200g S.R. flour

1 tsp mixed spice

Walnut halves

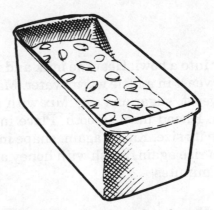

Mixture in a loaf tin with walnuts on top

Method:

Put all the ingredients, except the walnuts, into a bowl. Beat for 2 to 3 minutes. Spread the mixture evenly in a greased and lined 2 lb loaf tin and place walnuts on top. Bake at 325°F for $1\frac{1}{2}$ to $1\frac{3}{4}$ hours. Cool in the tin for 10 minutes. Turn it over and cool.

Yeast Buns

3 cups flour

Salt

$1\frac{1}{2}$ cups milk (luke warm)

1 tsp yeast

4 Tblsp margarine

1 egg

Method:

Sift together the flour and salt. Dissolve the yeast with little warm water. Rub the margarine into the flour. Make a well in the centre and mix in the yeast, milk and egg to form a soft dough. Knead on a lightly floured board until smooth. Place the dough into a clean greased bowl and allow to prove. Punch down the dough and knead again. Cut into balls and roll them out a little to make flat buns. Leave them on greased baking trays to prove. Brush with egg or milk. Bake at 375°F for 15 to 20 minutes, or until brown and cooked. Serve with hamburgers.

Mabumbunda: (Banana Bread)

12 ripe bananas

2 c maizemeal flour

Adding maize meal to ripe bananas

Portions of dough wrapped in banana leaves

Method:

Mash the ripe bananas and mix with enough maize meal to make a soft dough. Wrap portions of about 1 cup full in banana leaves or foil paper. Arrange them in a saucepan and fill it with water. Boil for $1\frac{1}{2}$ hours, or until they are firm to touch. Serve either hot or cold.

Cakes

Type of Cakes

Angel Cake

Boiled Fruit Cake

Cherry Slices

Carrot Cake

Cream Swiss Roll

Cinnamon Cake

Coffee Cake

Cherry Slices

Easter Gateaux

Jiffy Cake

Light Fruit Cake

Nutty Cakes

Orange Cake

Orange Frosting

Potato Cocoa Cake

Pear Cake

Peppermint Cake

Sponge Cake

Sunflower Shortcake

Treacle Cake

Angel cake

200 g sugar
150 g margarine
4 eggs
200 g flour

2 tbsp cornflour
1 tsp baking powder
$\frac{1}{4}$ cup milk
1 tsp vanilla essence

Method:

Cream sugar, vanilla and margarine until thick. Beat in the eggs and sift in the flour, baking powder and cornflour. Add the milk and essence and fold gently. Half fill the paper cake cases and bake at 375°F for 10 to 12 minutes, or until the cakes are cooked and browned.

Boiled Fruit Cake

1 cup black tea
3 tblsp margarine
3 tblsp sugar
1 cup sultanas or currants

$2\frac{1}{2}$ cups S.R. Flour
$\frac{1}{2}$ tsp cinnamon
$\frac{1}{4}$ tsp cloves (powdered)
1 egg

Method:

Boil the strained tea, fat, sugar and fruit for a few minutes. Let it cool. Sift the dry ingredients together, make a well and put the cooled mixture in it. Beat well and pour into a greased and lined cake tin. Bake at 350°F for 50 minutes, or until cookod.

Cherry Slices

200g butter or margarine
150g sugar
50g S.R. flour
50g mixed peels (grated)

50g cherries
4 eggs
2 tsp icing sugar

Method:

Cream margarine and sugar until light and fluffy. Beat in one egg at a time. Sift and fold in the flour, peels and the chopped fruits. Spread the mixture in a greased shallow tin. Bake at 350°F for 25 to 30 minutes. Dust with icing sugar and cut into slices. Cool and serve.

Carrot Cake

$1\frac{1}{2}$ cups flour

1 tsp baking powder

1 tsp bicarbonate of soda

1 cup sugar

1 tsp cinnamon

$\frac{1}{4}$ tsp salt

2 eggs

1 tsp of any essence

$\frac{3}{4}$ cup oil

1 cup grated carrots

Using a food mixer

Method:

Sift the dry ingredients together into a bowl. Add the rest of the ingredients and mix with a food mixer for 3 minutes. Grease an 8" cake tin and line it. Pour the mixture into this tin. Bake at 350°F for between 45 and 50 minutes, or until the cake is firm to touch and well browned. Cool and ice or serve without ice.

Cream Swiss Roll

4 eggs

$\frac{3}{4}$ c sugar

$\frac{3}{4}$ c plain wheat flour

$\frac{1}{2}$ tsp baking powder

1 tsp vanilla essence

Jam

Whipped cream

1 small piece

of cooking chocolate

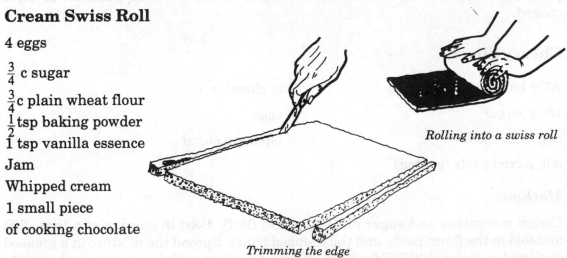

Rolling into a swiss roll

Trimming the edge

Method:

Break the eggs in a large bowl and add the sugar. Whip until the mixture is thick and lemon coloured. Sift in the flour and baking powder and gently fold in the whisked mixture. Add the essence and fold well. Pour the mixture into a greased and lined swiss roll tin. Bake at 375°F for 10 to 12 mins. Turn it out onto a wet clean tea towel. Trim the edges and spread the top with jam. Roll into a swiss roll and cool. When cold, cover the swiss roll with whipped cream and grate a little cooking chocolate on top of it. Serve or chill it first.

Cinnamon Cake

1 tblsp margarine

1 cup sugar

$1\frac{1}{2}$ cups flour

1 tsp baking powder

$\frac{1}{2}$ cup milk

2 eggs

2 tblsp cinnamon

Method:

Cream the margarine and sugar well. Stir in the eggs and put in the flour, baking powder and cinnamon. Add the milk and beat until smooth. Pour the mixture into a greased cake tin. Bake at 350°F for 40 to 45 minutes, or until cooked. Cool and serve.

Coffee Cake

$1\frac{1}{2}$ cups of flour

$\frac{1}{4}$ cup margarine

1 cup sugar

2 beaten eggs

1 tsp baking powder

A little milk

Filling:

$\frac{1}{2}$ cup brown sugar

1 tblsp butter

1 tblsp flour

$\frac{1}{2}$ cup nuts

$\frac{1}{2}$ tsp cinnamon

Section through baking tin showing layering

39

Method:

Cream margarine and sugar until fluffy. Add in the eggs and fold in the sifted flour with baking powder, alternating with milk. Keep aside.

Mix all the ingredients for the filling. Grease a baking tin and spread in a layer of the creamed mixture, alternating with a layer of filling and ending with a layer of filling. Bake at 350°F for 40 to 45 minutes, or until the cake is cooked.

Cherry Slices

100g margarine
75g sugar
120g self raising flour
20g mixed peels

20g cherries
2 eggs
1 tblsp icing sugar

Method:

Beat the sugar until white and soft. Beat in the eggs, one at a time. Sieve and fold in the flour and fruits. Pour into a baking tin. Bake at 350°F for 25 to 30 minutes. Sprinkle with icing sugar and cut into slices. Cool and serve.

Easter Gateaux Cake

200g margarine
4 eggs
1 tsp orange rind
1 tblsp orange juice
200g sugar
200g self raising flour
Filling:
    250g butter cream
    10 pcs ginger biscuits
    I cup chopped nuts
    $\frac{1}{2}$l whipped cream

Finished cakes

Method:

Cream fat and sugar until fluffy. Beat in one egg at a time. Sift the flour and gently fold it in with the orange rind and juice. Pour the mixture into two eight-inch sandwich tins. Bake at 350°F for 25 to 30 minutes and allow to cool.

Filling:

Cut the biscuits into halves. Use the butter cream to sandwich the cake together and to cover the sides. Roll it in chopped nuts and place it on a serving plate. Spread a little whipped cream on top and decorate the sides with the remaining cream. Arrange the biscuits on top. Crush one biscuit and sprinkle it on the cream.

Jiffy Cake

150g soft margarine
150g caster sugar
2 eggs

200g self raising flour
1 tsp baking powder
Fruit juice or 4 tsp milk

Method:

Place all ingredients in a large mixing bowl. Beat them hard for several minutes until well blended. Pour into a 7 inch greased and floured sandwich tin and bake for 1 hour at 350 to 375°F.

Light Fruit Cake

200g margarine
200g sugar
4 eggs
50g mixed peel

150g sultanas
1 tblsp treacle
1 tsp baking powder
250g flour

Method:

Cream fat and sugar until light and fluffy. Beat in one egg at a time. Mix in the fruits and treacle and lastly, fold in the dry ingredients. Pour into a greased and lined 10" cake tin. Bake at 300° F for 1 to $1\frac{1}{2}$ hours, or until the cake is cooked. Ice and serve when completely cold.

Nutty Cakes

150g S. R. Flour

75g chopped walnuts

125ml strong coffee

50g butter or margarine

50g sugar

1-2 eggs

Method:

Sift the flour and mix with the nuts, butter or margarine, coffee and sugar. Beat well before adding the egg. Half fill deep cake tins with the mixture. Bake at 375°F for 20 to 25 minutes.

Half-filled deep tins

Orange Cake

$2\frac{1}{2}$ cups flour

$1\frac{1}{2}$ cups sugar

1 tsp baking powder

A pinch of salt

$1\frac{1}{2}$ cups milk

$\frac{1}{2}$ cup margarine

3 eggs

1 tsp vanilla essence

1 cup chopped raisins

$\frac{1}{2}$ cup chopped nuts

1 tblsp grated orange peel

Applying icing on the covered cake

Method:

Heat the oven to 350°F. Grease and line an 8" cake tin. Beat all the ingredients together in a bowl slowly for 30 seconds and then fast for 3 minutes. Pour into tins and bake for 30 to 35 minutes, or until cooked. If an oblong pan is used, bake for 45 to 50 minutes. Cool and frost.

Orange Frosting

$\frac{1}{2}$ cup margarine, softened

$4\frac{1}{2}$ cups icing sugar

4-5 tblsp orange juice

1 tblsp orange peel, grated

Method:

Mix icing sugar and margarine. Beat in the juice and the rind. Use the mixture to sandwich and cover the cake.

42

Potato Cocoa Cake

1 cup cooked and mashed potatoes	50g cocoa
250g sugar	1 tsp baking powder
125g margarine	1 tsp cinnamon
4 eggs	1 tsp nutmeg
1 tsp vanilla essence	$\frac{1}{4}$ cup milk
200g plain flour	100g chopped nuts

Method:

Beat the margarine and sugar until fluffy. Add the eggs, one at a time, and mix well. Add in the essence and potatoes. Sift in the dry ingredients and stir in the milk, a little at a time, until the mixture becomes smooth. Stir in the nuts. Pour into a greased and lined baking tin. Bake at 350°F for 40 to 45 minutes. Let the cake stand for 5 minutes in the tin, turn out and cool.

Pear Cake

2 pears	175g flour
Juice of 1 lemon	50g ground nuts
100g sugar	1 tsp ginger
100g butter	1 tsp mixed spices
2 eggs	$\frac{1}{4}$ pt warm milk
1 tblsp treacle	1 tsp bicarbonate of soda

Method:

Peel and dice the pears and sprinkle them with lemon juice. Cream the butter and sugar until fluffy and stir in the eggs and the treacle. Sift the remaining dry ingredients together, except the bicarbonate of soda. Add the warmed milk to the bicarbonate of soda and pour into the creamed mixture, alternating with dry ingredients. Fold in the pears. Pour the mixture into a greased and lined tin. Bake at 180° for 45 to 50 minutes. Allow to cool and dredge with icing sugar.

Peppermint Cake

150g sugar	125g flour
2 level tblsp margarine	1 heaped tsp baking powder
2 eggs	1 tblsp cocoa
A few drops of vanilla essence	Peppermint butter cream

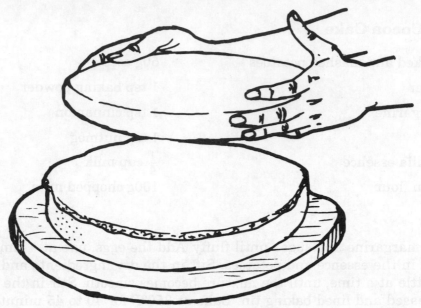

Sandwiching the cakes

Method:

Cream fat and sugar until fluffy. Add one egg at a time, then the essence and mix well. Sift in the flour, the baking powder and cocoa. Fold gently and pour into two sandwich tins. Bake at 400°F for 20 to 25 minutes. Cool it. Sandwich the two cakes with a thick layer of peppermint butter cream. Cover the top and sides with more cream. Decorate and Serve.

Sponge Cake

150g sugar   175g flour

150g margarine   1 tsp baking podwer

3-4 eggs

Applying jam before sandwiching

Method:

Cream fat and sugar until fluffy and light. Add one egg at a time and beat thoroughly. Sift in the flour and baking powder and fold gently until well blended. Pour into two greased and lined sandwich tins. Bake at 350°F for 20 to 25 minutes, or until cooked. Cool and sandwich together with jam.

Sunflower Shortcake

150g sieved flour

100g margarine

75g sugar

1 tin of peaches or apricots

250ml fruit juice

4 cherries

2 tsp cornflour

1 punnet of strawberries

A few almonds

Yellow food colour

Laid out fruit on cake

Method:

Cream fat and sugar until fluffy. Add in the sieved flour and mix well. Press the dough into an 8" greased sandwich tin. Bake at 375°F for 25 to 30 minutes. Cool it. Drain the peaches and measure out 250ml of the juice. Keep aside one whole peach and slice the rest. Arrange the sliced fruit around the edges of the pastry overlapping each other. Place the uncut peach in the centre. Cut the strawberries into quarters and arrange them around the centre. Blend the cornflour and juice in a pan and boil. Stir in a little yellow food colour and coat the fruit with this mixture. Slice the almonds and stick them into the fruit in the centre. Decorate with the cherries and serve.

Treacle Cake

200g sugar

100g margarine

2 eggs

200g flour

2 tsp baking flour

1 tsp mixed spices

2 Tblsp treacle syrup

125ml milk

Method:

Cream margarine and sugar until light and fluffy. Add the eggs one at a time. Sift in the flour, spices and baking powder and fold them in gently, adding the treacle and the milk. Pour the mixture into a greased tin and bake at 350°F for 70 to 75 minutes, or until cooked.

Chicken

Varieties of Chicken Dishes

Baked Chicken

Batter Fried Chicken

Chicken with Cashewnuts

Casserole of Chicken and Peas

Chicken with Chapatis

Chicken in Coconut

Chicken Pies

Chicken Pizza

Chicken Rolls

Chicken Stew

Chicken in Tomatoes

Chicken and Ugali

Continental Chicken

Fried Chicken with Fried Onions

Grilled Marinated Chicken

Grilled Spiced Chicken

Nutty Chicken

Roast Egg Stuffed Chicken

Roast Stuffed Chicken

Spiced Chicken Stew

Baked Chicken

1 chicken, jointed	$\frac{1}{4}$ kg peas
$2\frac{1}{2}$ c Milk,	2 large tomatoes
2 tblsp flour	$\frac{1}{2}$ c cream
salt, pepper	Fat for frying
4 tblsp margarine	
1 onion (chopped)	

Method:

Dip the pieces of chicken into milk and then into seasoned flour. Fry them in melted fat until brown. Place them in a casserole. Fry the onion and peas for 2 to 3 minutes before adding in the tomatoes and seasoning. Pour the milk and the cream over the chicken. Cook from the lower rack of an oven at 350°F for $1\frac{1}{2}$ hours.

Batter Fried Chicken

1 chicken	*Batter*
Salt, pepper	1 cup flour
2 tblsp flour	1 tsp baking powder
Oil for frying	1 tsp salt
	A pinch of pepper
	1 egg
	1 cup milk
	$\frac{1}{2}$ cup oil

Tossing the chicken in seasoned flour and placing in hot oil

Method:

Sift all the dry ingredients for the batter into a bowl. Beat in the egg, milk and oil until smooth.

Cut the chicken into pieces, toss into seasoned flour and dip into the batter. Fry in hot oil until cooked and well browned. Drain the oil on soft paper and serve with potatoes, the vegetables in season and gravy.

Chicken with Cashewnuts

1 chicken

Juice of $\frac{1}{2}$ a lemon

2 onions

1 kg tomatoes

1 cup cashewnuts

3-4 tblsp fat

Salt, pepper

Mashed potatoes

Method:

Cut the chicken into serving pieces. Boil it with water, salt, pepper and lemon juice until tender. Drain off the stock and keep it aside. Chop the onions and tomatoes. Pound the nuts with a little water to make a paste. Heat the fat and fry the onions until soft. Add the tomatoes, cover and cook until soft. Add the nut paste and the chicken. Pour in enough stock to make a thick sauce. Cover and simmer for a few minutes. Serve with mashed potatoes.

Caserole of Chicken and Peas

Chicken, jointed

50g flour

Seasoning

Grated lemon rind

Lemon juice

2-3 tblsp oil

2 onions

4 tomatoes

1 clove garlic

$\frac{1}{2}$ pt stock

10 oz fresh peas

Crushing garlic

Method:

Remove the giblet from the Chicken. Simmer the giblet with about 200ml of water to make a good stock. Coat the joints of chieken with the flour blended with seasoning and grated lemon rind. Fry the joints in hot oil until golden brown. Put them on a plate. Fry the chopped onions and crushed garlic and simmer them for 15 minutes. Put the sauce and the peas into a caserole and place the joints on top. Cover the dish and cook for 45 minutes at 350° F.

Chicken with Chapatis

2 tblsp fat	1 tsp paprika powder
1 chicken (jointed)	1 tblsp tomato paste
2 onions (sliced)	1 cup yoghurt or sour milk
2 cloves of garlic (crushed)	1 cup water
1 tsp. ginger (crushed)	Juice of $\frac{1}{2}$ a lemon
Salt, pepper	Whole chillies (optional)
1 tsp tumeric	

Method:

Heat the fat and fry the pieces of chicken until golden brown. Keep them aside. In the same frying pan, fry the onion until golden brown. Add the garlic, ginger, and seasonings and fry for a while. Add the tomato puree and yoghurt. Put back the chicken and pour in water. Cover and simmer until the chicken is soft. Sprinkle in the lemon juice. Whole chillies are optional. Serve hot.

Chapatis:

2 cups flour	About $\frac{1}{2}$ pt of warm water
2 tblsp oil	Extra oil
A little salt	

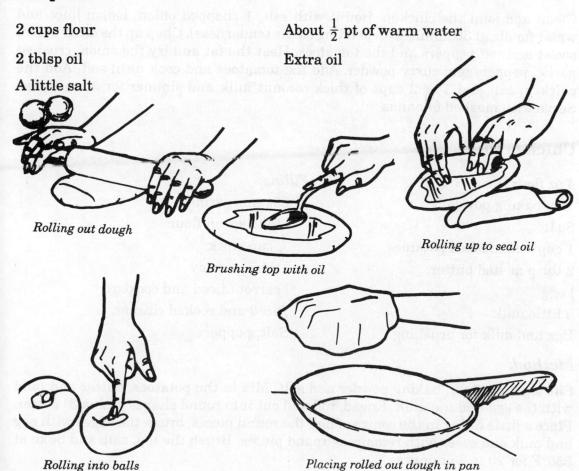

Rolling out dough

Brushing top with oil

Rolling up to seal oil

Rolling into balls

Placing rolled out dough in pan

49

Method:

Sift the flour and salt into bowl. Add the oil and water and knead to form a soft dough. Cut into balls the size of a large egg. Roll out to about the size of a saucer. Brush the top with oil. Roll up to seal the oil and shape into a round ball. Roll out again very thinly and cook both sides on a heated dry frying pan for two minutes. Brush both sides with oil and cook until brown.

Chicken in Coconut

1 chicken	2 tblsp fat
2 large onions	Juice of 1 lemon
3 cloves of garlic	Milk from 1 coconut
1 red pepper	Salt
1-2 sweet peppers	4 tomatoes
1 tsp curry powder	

Method:

Clean and joint the chicken. Boil it with salt, 1 chopped onion, lemon juice and water for about 30 minutes (depending on the tenderness). Chop up the other onion, sweet and red peppers and the tomatoes. Heat the fat and fry the onion, crushed garlic, peppers and curry powder. Add the tomatoes and cook until soft. Add the chicken, salt and 1 or 2 cups of thick coconut milk and simmer for 30 minutes. Serve with mashed bananas.

Chicken Pies

4 oz flour	*Filling:-*
1tsp baking powder	25g margarine
Salt	1 tablespoon flour
1 cup cold mashed potatoes	$\frac{1}{2}$ cup stock
2 tblsp melted butter	1 tblsp parsley
1 egg	1 carrot (diced and cooked)
a little milk	Diced and cooked chicken
Egg and milk for brushing	Salt, pepper

Method:

Sift together flour, baking powder and salt. Mix in the potatoes, butter and bind with the egg and the milk. Knead, roll and cut into round shapes with a 3" cutter. Place a little filling in the centre of half the round pieces, brush the edges with egg and milk and cover with remaining round pieces. Brush the top, snip and bake at 350°F for 20 to 25 minutes.

Placing filling on the dough

Covering with another round piece and sealing

Brushing the edges with eggs and milk

Filling:

Melt the margarine, add flour and cook the flour in it for two minutes. Pour in the stock and stir until thick. Mix with the remaining ingredients and use to fill as required.

Chicken Pizza

1 small cooked chicken	**Dough**
2 sliced tomatoes	200g flour
1 egg	4 level tsp baking powder
125ml cream or milk	Pinch of salt
Salt, pepper	25g butter
100g cheese, grated	125ml milk
Sprigs of parsley	

Method:

Pressing dough into baking tray

Sieve together the flour, the baking powder and the salt. Rub in the butter and bind with milk to a fairly soft dough. Press it onto the base of a shallow oblong baking tray. Cover the surface of the dough with tomato slices and chopped chicken. Pour over them the lightly beaten egg with cream, salt and pepper. Sprinkle the cheese on top. Bake at 425°F for 15 to 20 minutes. Serve hot, garnished with sprigs of parsley and pieces of tomatoes.

Chicken Rolls

2 onions
1 tblsp fat
 Salt, pepper
1 tblsp chopped parsley
1 cup fresh breadcrumbs
A little lemon juice
4 - 6 chicken breasts
Extra melted fat

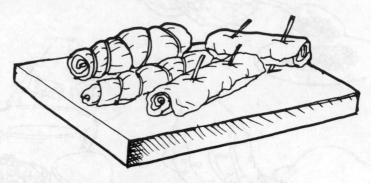

Rolls secured with string and toothpicks

Method:

Heat the fat and fry the onions with parsley, salt, pepper, bread crumbs and juice. Mix well. Remove bones from the breasts and flatten out the meat with a rolling pin. Place a little stuffing on each breast. Roll them up and tie or secure with wooden sticks. Place on a baking tray and brush with extra melted fat. Bake at 350°F' for 25 to 30 minutes, or until cooked and browned.

Chicken Stew

1 chicken	$\frac{1}{4}$ kg. tomatoes
2 tblsp fat	1 tsp curry powder
2 onions, chopped	4 potatoes, quartered
2 cloves of garlic	1 lt water or stock
1 bunch chopped dania	2 whole chillies
1 sweet pepper, diced	

Method:

Cut the chicken into serving pieces. Heat the fat and fry the onions and garlic until brown. Add the chopped dania, sweet pepper and tomatoes. Cook until the tomatoes are soft. Add the curry powder, chicken and potatoes. Toss well and, lastly, add water, salt and chillies. Cover and simmer until the chicken is tender. Serve with ugali.

Chicken in Tomatoes

1 chicken	2 cloves of garlic, crushed
Salt, paprika pepper	4 large tomatoes, chopped
4 tblsp oil	$\frac{1}{2}$ c water
1 onion	1 bunch chopped dania

Method:

Clean and dry the pieces of chicken. Season with salt and paprika. Heat the oil and brown all sides of the chicken. Add the onion and garlic and cook until the onions are soft. Add the tomatoes and lemon juice. Cover and cook until the tomatoes are soft. Pour in the water and simmer until the chicken is cooked. Serve with rice or potatoes and sprinkle the chopped dania or parsley on top of the chicken.

Chicken and Ugali

1 chicken	1 large chopped onion
Salt, pepper	2 cloves of garlic, crushed
Juice of 1 lemon	1 tblsp chopped dania
1 tblsp flour	1 or $1\frac{1}{2}$ c stock
$\frac{1}{2}$ c oil	

Method:

Rub the pieces of chicken with salt and lemon juice and toss them in seasoned flour. Heat the oil and fry the chicken until golden brown. Keep aside. Drain off the oil from the pan and fry the onion, garlic and dania before adding the tomatoes. Cook until soft. Add the chicken, seasoning and stock. Simmer until the chicken is cooked.

Ugali Balls

$2\frac{1}{2}$ c maizemeal	A knob of butter
2 c water	1 egg
Salt	Oil for frying

Cooking ugali

Method:

Cook the ugali in salted water until done. Add a knob of butter and shape into balls. Dip them into the beaten egg and fry in hot oil until brown. Serve with the chicken.

Continental Chicken

1 large chicken

$2\frac{1}{2}$ cups water

Salt, pepper

1 onion

6 cloves of garlic

1 egg

$\frac{1}{2}$ cup breadcrumbs

Oil for frying

2 slices of pineapple

Sauce:

1-2 cups stock

1 tblsp corn flour

$\frac{3}{4}$ cup tomato paste or $\frac{1}{4}$ kilo tomatoes

Salt, chilli pepper

Boiled spaghetti

1 cup cooked peas

Parsley

Method:

Cut the chicken into pieces. Cook them in water with salt, grated onion and chopped garlic. Remove the pieces and dip them into the beaten egg, roll into breadcrumbs and fry both sides until light brown in colour. Cut the pineaple into small pieces. Cook together the stock, salt, cornflour, tomato sauce, paste and pepper, stirring until thick. Mix in the pineapple slices and remove from the heat.

Arrange the chicken pieces on a serving plate and surround it with hot spaghetti and peas. Pour the sauce over them and garnish with parsley.

Fried Chicken with Fried Onion Rings

1 young chicken

$\frac{1}{2}$ cup flour

1 tsp salt

1 tsp paprika

$\frac{1}{4}$ tsp pepper

Oil for frying

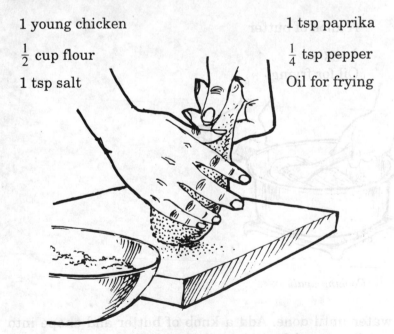

Coating the chicken with seasonings

Method:

Cut the chicken into pieces. Dry them with a cloth. Mix the flour with the seasonings and coat the chicken with it.

Heat the oil and fry the chicken until cooked and crisp. For a tough chicken, add a little water into the pan and cover. Simmer for 30 to 40 minutes.

Fried Onion Rings

2-3 large onions

$\frac{1}{2}$ cup water

1 egg

$\frac{3}{4}$ cup flour

$\frac{1}{2}$ tsp baking powder

$\frac{1}{2}$ tsp salt

Oil for frying

Slicing the onion

Method:

Peel and slice the onions and seperate them into rings. Mix the flour, salt, baking powder, egg and water then beat into a smooth batter. Dip the rings in the batter, allowing the excess batter to drip into the bowl. Fry in hot oil until brown. Serve with the chicken.

Grilled Marinated Chicken

1 chicken	1 tsp ginger, paprika
1 large onion	A little yoghurt
3 cloves of garlic	Salt
2 tblsp lemon juice	Flour
1 tsp powdered cumin seeds	Oil for frying

Method:

Clean and cut the chicken into serving pieces. Mix the minced onion, garlic, ginger, lemon juice, chilli powder, cumin seeds and yoghurt. Rub this mixture on the chicken. Allow to marinate for a few hours (4 hrs for a tough chicken and less time for a tender chicken). Heat the oil, dip the pieces in seasoned flour and fry in the hot oil until cooked and browned. Serve with chips and salads. The chicken may be grilled instead of being fried.

Grilled Spiced Chicken

1 chicken	1 tsp cumin seeds powder
1 large onion	1 tsp ginger, crushed
1 tsp chilli powder	$\frac{1}{2}$ c yoghurt
3 cloves of garlic	salt
2 tblsp lemon juice	Oil for frying

Method:

Clean and cut the chicken into 4 pieces. Chop finely or mince the onion and garlic. Mix the ginger, lemon juice, salt, chilli powder, cumin seeds, yoghurt, onion and garlic and rub it all over the pieces. Allow to marinate for at least 4 hours. Heat the oil in a pan and fry the chicken until brown and cooked. Serve with potato chips and a green salad.

The chicken can be grilled instead of being fried.

Nutty Chicken

1 chicken	25g flour
1 egg	$\frac{1}{4}$ lt milk
Salt and pepper	50g groundnuts, chopped
$1\frac{1}{2}$ c soft breadcrumbs	1 tblsp parsley (chopped)
$\frac{1}{2}$ c oil	Mashed potatoes
25g margarine	

Method:

Cut the chicken into pieces and boil in water until soft. Drain and cool. Beat the egg and dip the chicken pieces in it. Coat with breadcrumbs and fry in hot oil until brown. Keep warm.

Meanwhile, heat the margarine and cook the flour in it until thick. Pour in the milk in thirds, stirring all the time. Cook until smooth and cooked. Remove from the heat and add the nuts and parsley. Garnish the chicken with potatoes and pour the sauce over it.

Roast Egg Stuffed Chicken

1 roasting chicken	Salt and pepper
Stuffing:	3 tblsp chopped parsley
1 Cup soft breadcrumbs	1 beaten egg
3 onions, grated	2 hard boiled eggs
3 tblsp butter	Grated rind and juice of 1 lemon

Method:

Heat the butter and fry the grated onions, add the breadcrumbs and parsley and mix well. Remove from the heat and add the seasoning, beaten egg, lemon rind and juice. Spread the seasoning and butter on the cleaned chicken. Fill the chicken with half the stuffing, followed by shelled boiled eggs, ending with the remaining stuffing. Skewer the end and tie the legs firmly in position. Place it in a roasting tin and bake at 375°F for 20 minutes for every pound, plus an extra 20 minutes, or until the chicken is well browned. Serve with potatoes, green peas and gravy.

Roast Stuffed Chicken

150g soft breadcrumbs	1 tblsp parsley, chopped
2 hard boiled eggs	1 egg
50g fat	1 chicken
1 onion (chopped)	seasoning

Method:

Chop the eggs, mix with breadcrumbs, fat, seasoning, parsley, onion and bind with a beaten egg. Put the stuffing into the chicken, brush with fat and place in a roasting tin. Bake at 425°F for 40 to 50 minutes if the chicken is young. You can also wrap the chicken in foil and roast for 1 hour 25 minutes at 350°F. Open up the tail and bake for another 11 to 15 minutes. Serve with roast potatoes and boiled vegetables with gravy.

Spiced Chicken Stew

1 large chicken	1 bay leaf
2 large onions	Pinch of powdered or fresh ginger
3 carrots	A little pepper
2 cloves of garlic	Salt
1 sweet pepper, chopped	Juice of $\frac{1}{2}$ lemon
2 tblsp fat	$\frac{3}{4}$ pt stock or water
2 tblsp tomato paste	$\frac{1}{2}$ oz fat
$\frac{1}{2}$ oz flour	3 tblsp water

Method:

Cut the chicken into pieces. Peel and slice the onions and carrots and crush the garlic. Heat the fat and fry the chicken until well browned. Add the vegetables and fry until soft. Stir in the tomato paste, bay leaf, seasoning, spices and the stock. Cook on medium heat until the chicken is tender. Add the lemon juice. Mix the fat, flour and water and pour into the stew, stirring until well thickened.

Fish

Fish Dishes:

Masala Jumbo Prawns

Fish Balls

Fish Banana Balls

Fish Cakes

Fish Flan

Fish and Chips

Fish Pilau (Zanzibar)

Fish Pizza

Fish in Tomatoes

Fish Ugali Patties

Fish and Vegetable Stew

Fish in Rice

Fish with Groundnuts

Fried Fish with Bananas

Fried Fish Cocktail

Potato, Fish and Corn Casserole

Stewed Fish

Masala Jumbo Prawns

1 kg Jumbo prawns

1-2 green chillies

1 tblsp cumin seeds

1 tsp curry powder

$\frac{1}{2}$ tsp ginger

2 cloves of garlic

Salt

1 bunch of dania

1 tblsp lemon juice

Oil for frying

Splitting prawns

Method:

Remove the shells from the prawns. Clean and split them on the outer edges. Pound all the other ingredients together and stuff each prawn. Allow them to marinate for 30 minutes. Fry in shallow oil until cooked. Serve with fried rice.

Fish Balls

$\frac{1}{2}$ kg fish fillet

$1\frac{1}{2}$ cups mashed potatoes

2 tblsp chopped parsley

1 egg

1 c breadcrumbs

Oil for frying

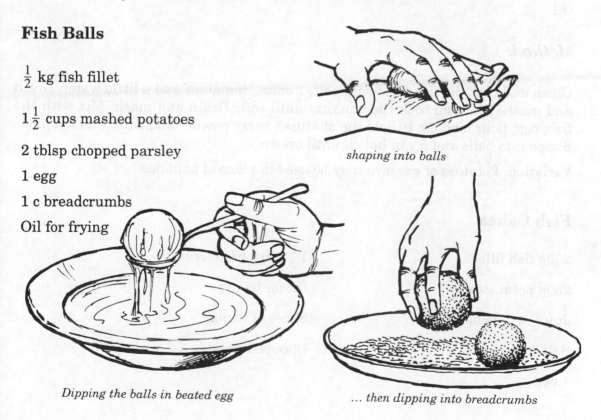

shaping into balls

Dipping the balls in beated egg

... then dipping into breadcrumbs

Method:

Boil the fillet, remove the bones and mash it. Mix with the potatoes, parsley and seasoning. Shape into balls, dip into the beaten egg and into the breadcrumbs. Fry in hot oil until well browned. Drain and serve.

Fish, Banana Balls

$\frac{1}{2}$ kg fish fillet

Salt

2 onions, chopped

2 chopped tomatoes

$\frac{1}{2}$ c water

10 green cooking bananas

1 egg

2 tblsp flour

1 tsp curry powder

Juice of 1 lemon

Oil

Draining the bananas

Method:

Clean and cook the fish fillet with salt, 1 onion, tomatoes and a little water. Drain and mash. Peel and cook the bananas until soft. Drain and mash. Mix with the fish, egg, flour (enough to hold the mixture), curry powder and a little lemon juice. Shape into balls and fry in hot oil until brown.

Variation: Potatoes or cassava may be used in place of bananas.

Fish Cakes

250g fish fillet

250g potataoes

Juice of $\frac{1}{2}$ lemon

Salt, pepper

1 egg

$1\frac{1}{2}$ c dry breadcrumbs

Oil for frying

Slices of lemon

Chopped parsley

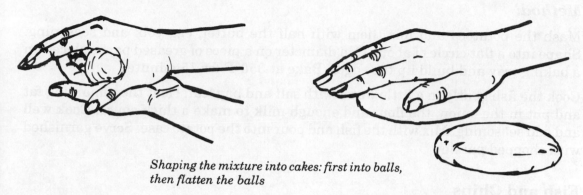

Shaping the mixture into cakes: first into balls,
then flatten the balls

Method:

Boil the fish in salted water. Mash it. Boil the potatoes. Mix the fish with mashed potatoes, lemon juice, pepper and salt. Shape into cakes. Cover the cakes with the egg and breadcrumbs. Fry in hot oil until cooked. Serve with lemons and parsley.

Fish Flan

$\frac{1}{2}$ kg boiled potatoes	Bay leaf
50g butter	25g flour
1 egg (separated)	1 c milk
$\frac{1}{4}$ kg cooked fish	Salt, pepper
$\frac{1}{2}$ small onion	1 tblsp chopped parsley

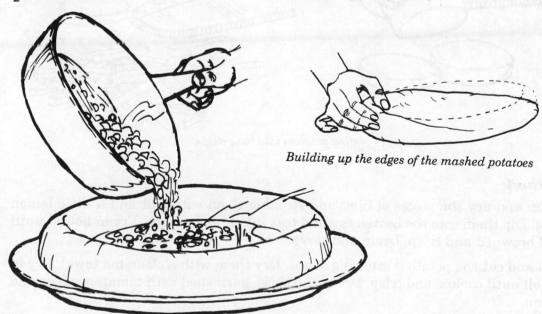

Building up the edges of the mashed potatoes

Pouring fish into the potato case

Method:

Mash the potatoes and mix them with half the butter, egg yolk and seasoning. Shape into a flat circle of about 7" in diameter on a piece of greased paper placed on a baking tray and build up the edges. Bake at 350°F for 15 minutes.

Cook the fish gently in a little water with salt and bay leaf. Heat the remaining fat and put in the onion, the flour and enough milk to make a thick sauce. Cook well and add seasoning. Mix with the fish and pour into the potato case. Serve garnished with chopped parsley.

Fish and Chips

4 pieces of fish fillet	2 lemons
Salt	Oil for frying
1 egg	1 kg of potatoes
1 c dry breadcrumbs	Tomato wedges

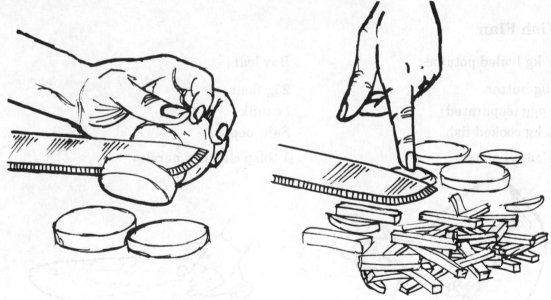

Stages in cutting potatoes into long strips

Method:

Clean and dry the pieces of fillet and sprinkle them with salt and a little lemon juice. Dip them into the beaten egg and toss into breadcrumbs. Fry in hot oil until well browned and crisp. Drain and serve.

Peel and cut the potatoes into long strips. Dry them with a clean tea towel. Fry in hot oil until cooked and crisp. Drain and serve garnished with tomato wedges and lemon.

Fish Pilau (Zanzibar)

4 tblsp oil	1 tsp garlic
1 large onion, chopped	2 chillies
$\frac{1}{4}$ kg potatoes, quartered	$\frac{1}{2}$ kg king fish (cubed)
Salt	2 c thin coconut milk
1 c chopped tomatoes	Juice of 1 lemon
1 tblsp cumin seeds	1 c thick coconut milk
1 tblsp dania	Rice
$\frac{1}{4}$ tsp tumeric powder	

Method:

Heat the oil in a saucepan and fry the chopped onion until light brown. Add the potatoes and salt and cook for five minutes. Add the tomatoes, dania, tumeric, chillies and toss well. Add the fish and about two cups of thin coconut milk. Cook until the potatoes are done. Add the lemon juice and about 1 cup of thick coconut milk. Cook for a further 5 minutes.

Fish Pizza

300g S.R flour

Salt

50g butter

About 12 tblsp milk

2 eggs

$\frac{1}{2}$ kg cooked fish fillet

2-3 tomatoes, sliced

A little oil

Covering fish with tomato slices

Method:

Sift the flour and salt into a mixing bowl. Rub in the butter. Mix the milk and the eggs and cut the mixture into the flour. Gather the dough and spread it evenly into a greased tin. Spread the fish over it and cover with tomato slices. Pour any remaining milk and egg mixture on top. Bake at 400°F for 30 minutes.

Fish in Tomatoes

1 kg king fish	1 cup stock
$\frac{1}{2}$ kg tomatoes	1 tsp cornflour
2 onions	Seasoning – salt, pepper
2 cloves of garlic	

Method:

Clean the fish and wrap it in foil paper. Boil it in salted water for 15 to 20 minutes. Drain off the liquid and reserve one cup. Peel and chop the onions and tomatoes and crush the garlic. Simmer them in the reserved liquid with seasoning until the tomatoes are cooked. Thicken with cornflour. Arrange the fish on a platter and pour the mixture over it. Serve with boiled potatoes and carrots.

Fish Ugali Patties

$2\frac{1}{2}$ c maizemeal	1 chopped onion
2 c boiling water	1 tblsp oil
Salt	1-2 eggs
1 cup cooked flaked fish	Oil for frying

Method:

Cook the maizemeal in salted boiling water until ready and soft. Heat the fat and fry the onion and mix with the cooked ugali. Add the egg and make into patties. Fry both sides in shallow oil until brown.

Fish and Vegetable Stew

$\frac{1}{2}$ kg king fish	1 sliced brinjal
3 tablespoons oil	4 chopped tomatoes
3 onions (sliced)	A little water
1 sliced sweet pepper	Salt and pepper

Method:

Clean and cut the fish into pieces. Heat the oil and fry the onions until soft. Add the pepper, tomatoes, brinjal and lastly, the fish. Season well and pour in the water. Cover and simmer for just long enough to cook the fish and the vegetables. Serve with potatoes.

Fish in Rice

2 large onions, chopped
2 c rice
2 chopped tomatoes
1 c peas

2 small sweet peppers
4 c stock
$\frac{1}{2}$ tsp yellow food colour
$\frac{1}{2}$ kg fish fillet

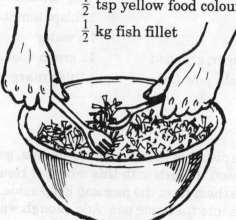
Tossing the mixture

Method:

Heat the oil and fry the onion and rice until transparent. Add in the tomatoes and cook until soft. Add the peas and chopped peppers and toss well. Season and add the stock, colouring and fish. Cover and simmer until rice is cooked.

Fish with Groundnuts

1 large fish
Salt
1 tsp curry powder
1 cup of oil

2 small onions
1 c tomatoes (chopped)
2 tblsp groundnut paste
1 cup water

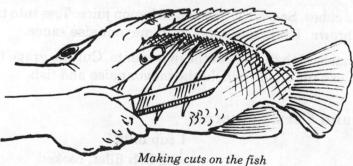
Making cuts on the fish

Method:

Clean the fish and make $\frac{1}{2}$ inch deep cuts across it. Season it with salt, curry powder and fry in hot oil until crisp and cooked.

In a clean pan, heat the oil and fry the onion until soft. Add the tomatoes and groundnut paste and cook until the tomatoes are soft. Add the seasoning and a little water at a time and stir until the sauce is thick. Serve with the fish and ugali.

Fried Fish with Bananas

$\frac{1}{2}$ kg fish (preferably King fish)

2 onions

3 cloves of garlic

Salt

1 small piece of ginger, crushed

1 tsp paprika or chilli powder

1 bunch dania

$\frac{1}{2}$ c oil

$\frac{1}{2}$ kg tomatoes

1 tblsp tomato paste

1 c water

12 green cooking bananas

1 tblsp margarine

Method:

Clean and wipe the pieces of fish. Pound the onions, garlic, salt, ginger, paprika and dania together. Season the fish with this mixture. Heat a little oil and fry the pieces until crisp. Remove them from the pan and keep aside. Pour the remaining mixture, tomatoes and puree into the same pan. Add enough water to make a thick gravy and cook until thick. Serve with boiled, mashed bananas mixed with margarine.

Fried Fish Cocktail

$\frac{1}{2}$ kg fish fillet

Juice of 1 lemon

Salt, pepper

1 tblsp flour

1c mayonnaise

1 onion (chopped)

1 tblsp chopped parsley

2 grape fruits

Oil for frying

Method:

Cut the fish into cubes. Season with salt and lemon juice. Toss into the flour and fry in hot oil until brown. Drain and serve with mayonnaise sauce.

Mix the mayonnaise with the rest of the ingredients. Cut the grape fruits, scoop out the insides and use the shells to hold the mayonnaise and fish.

Potato Fish and Corn Casserole

4 Potatoes

2 tblsp butter

1 chopped onion

1 chopped sweet pepper

2 tblsp margarine

1 tblsp flour

Salt, pepper

1 tsp paprika

1 cup milk

$\frac{1}{2}$ kg fish fillet, cooked

1 cup cooked corn

2 tblsp fresh breadcrumbs

1 tblsp fresh breadcrumbs

1 tblsp melted butter

Chopped parsley

Pouring mixture over potatoes

Method:

Peel and slice the potatoes and arrange them in a greased casserole. Heat the margarine and fry the onion and pepper until tender. Add the flour, salt and paprika and, gradually, the milk. Cook until smooth, stirring constantly until thick. Add the corn and flaked fish. Pour this mixture over the potatoes. Toss the crumbs into melted butter and sprinkle them into the casserole. Bake at 350°F for 30 to 40 minutes or until the potatoes are cooked. Serve garnished with parsley.

Stewed Fish

$\frac{1}{2}$ kg fish

2 cloves of garlic (crushed)

1 tblsp finely chopped dania

1 c tomatoes

Salt

$\frac{1}{2}$ c water

Juice of 1 lemon

Method:

Clean and scale the fish. Remove the head if not preferred. Place the fish in a pan, sprinkle with salt and add the tomatoes, garlic, dania and a little water. Cook slowly on a low fire until the fish is cooked. Add a little lemon juice and serve.

Fruit dishes

Banana Drop Doughnuts

Banana Puffs

Fruit Juice Punch

Fruit Fritters

Fruit Scones

Mint Delight

Pawpaw Jam

Special Fruit Drink

Banana Drop Doughnuts

2 ripe bananas

$\frac{1}{4}$ c sugar

$\frac{1}{2}$ tsp baking powder

1 egg

3 tblsp flour

1 tsp cardamon powder

$\frac{1}{2}$ c milk

Oil for frying

Dropping spoonfuls of batter into hot oil

Method:

Mash the bananas and mix them with sugar, baking powder, egg, flour and cardamon. Add enough milk to form a thick batter. Drop spoonfuls of the batter into hot oil and fry until golden brown in colour. Drain and serve.

Banana Puffs

100g flour

50g maizemeal flour

75g sugar

1 egg

1 tsp baking powder

1 c milk

2 ripe bananas

Oil for frying

Method:

Sift together the flour, maizemeal, baking powder and the sugar. Make a well in the centre and mix in the egg and enough milk to form a thick batter. Peel and slice the bananas and mix them with the batter. Heat the oil and fry spoonfuls of the mixture in hot oil until golden brown in colour. Drain on soft paper and serve.

Fruit Juice Punch

5ml black tea

750ml fruit juice

300ml ginger ale

Sugar to taste

Ice cubes

Slices of lemon

Method:

Place the tea, fruit juice and ginger ale
in a bowl. Stir in the sugar until it dissolves.
Stir in the ice cubes. Pour the drink into glasses
and place a slice of lemon in each glass. Serve immediately.

Fruit Fritters

4 tblsp flour	1 tsp sugar
2 eggs	1 cup milk
$\frac{1}{2}$ tsp baking powder	Oil for frying
1 tblsp Oil	Soft fruit, eg. bananas, mangoes, apples

Dropping spoonfuls of fruit mixture into hot oil

Method:

Sift together the flour and the baking powder. Add the sugar, oil, eggs and milk to
the flour and beat to a smooth batter. Cut the fruit and put it into the batter. Drop
spoonfuls of the mixture into hot oil and fry until golden brown. Drain with soft
paper and Serve.

70

Fruit Scones

$\frac{1}{2}$ kg flour

1 tsp baking powder

75 g margarine

2 tblsp sugar

250ml milk

$\frac{1}{2}$ c currants

1 egg for brushing

Method:

Sift the flour and baking powder into a bowl. Rub in the margarine and add the sugar and fruits. Pour in the milk to form a moist dough. Knead lightly. Roll and and cut into scones. Brush the tops with the egg and bake at 425°F for 10 to 15 minutes, or until brown.

Mint Delight

1 lt milk

4 tblsp sugar

$1\frac{1}{2}$ tsp peppermint essence

5-6 drops of green food colouring

$\frac{1}{2}$ lt ice cream

Maraschino cherries and pieces of pineapple

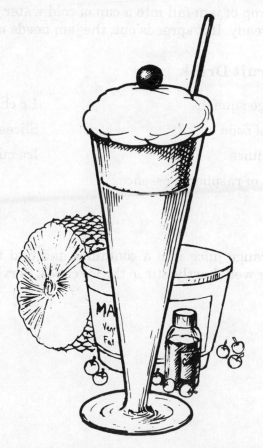

Method:

Pour the milk into a large bowl or jug. Add the sugar, peppermint and colouring and stir to blend well. Pour into glasses and top with a scoop of ice cream. Garnish with maraschino cherries and pieces of pineapple.

Pawpaw Jam

3 cups ripe paw paw pulp

3 cups sugar

$\frac{1}{2}$ cup lemon juice

Method:

Boil all the ingredients until thick. Stir frequently. Cool and pour into jars.

To Test for Jam Thickness:

(1) Drop a little hot jam onto a cold plate and let it cool. If it sets and the surface wrinkles when touched, the jam is ready.

(2) Let a little jam fall off a spoon. It should drop whole and not drip off the spoon.

(3) Let a drop of jam fall into a cup of cold water. If the drop remains whole, the jam is ready. If it spreads out, the jam needs more cooking.

Special Fruit Drink

750ml orange squash

6-8 bottles of soda

2 cups lime juice

A few drops of raspberry essence

1 c chopped cherries

Slices of lemon for garnishing

Ice cubes

Method:

Pour the orange juice into a container and add the lime juice, soda, fruits and essence. Stir well. Lastly, stir in the ice cubes. Serve in glasses topped with slices of lemon.

Meat

Varieties of Meat Dishes

Baked Meat Cakes
Bananas in Groundnut Sauce
Bananas with Minced Beef
Bananas with Meat
Bananas with Tripe
Beef Stew with Rice Rings
Beef in Beer
Beef and Cheese Delight
Beef and Cheese Slices
Beef and Noodles Casserole
Beef Rolls in Tomatoes
Beef Soup
Beef Stew
Biriani
Meat, Cheese Pie
Cold Beef
Corned Beef Cakes
Cutlets
Dried Meat Stew
Spiced Fried Meat
Fried Meat Rolls
Fried Mutton
Kebabs
Liver and Potato Casserole
Lunchtime Meat Loaf
Marinated Steak
Marinated Steak Cocktail
Meatballs with Vegetables
Meat with Corn Dish
Meat Loaf
Meat Filled Pancakes
Meat Stew
Meat with Scones Topping
Meatballs in a Nest
Meat Ring with Corn
Meat and Potato Chops
Minced Beef and Peas Pie
Minced Meat Pinwheels
Mishkaki
Mutton Curry
Nyama Choma
Oxtail Stew
Grilled Marinated Mutton
Samosas
Skillet Dinner
Steak in Gravy

Baked Meat Cakes

$\frac{1}{2}$ kg minced beef

4 small carrots, grated

6 Tblsp soft breadcrumbs

1 small onion, grated

1 egg

Seasoning

Melted margarine

Dried breadcrumbs

Method:

Combine the meat, carrots, soft breadcrumbs, onion, egg and seasoning. Mix well. Divide into six portions, roll in margarine and breadcrumbs. Place on baking trays and bake at 350°F for 40 minutes. Serve with potatoes topped with onion sauce and a sprig of parsley.

Bananas in Groundnuts

1 tblsp fat

1 onion (chopped)

2 tomatoes (chopped)

1 tsp curry powder

$1\frac{1}{2}$ c pounded groundnuts

2-3 c water

Salt

12 green cooking bananas

Method:

Heat the fat and fry the onions until soft. Add the tomatoes and then the curry powder. Add in the groundnuts and cook for a while. Pour in the water and add the seasoning. Peel and cut the bananas and add them into the stew. Simmer until the bananas are cooked. Mash together and keep warm.

Bananas with Minced Beef

1 tblsp oil

1 onion (chopped)

2 tomatoes (chopped)

$\frac{1}{4}$ kg minced beef

$\frac{1}{2}$ c peas

$\frac{1}{2}$ c diced carrots

12 green cooking bananas

1 tblsp mchuzi mix

2 c water

Method:

Heat the oil and fry the onion until light brown in colour. Add the tomatoes and cook until soft and then the meat until brown. Add the peas, carrots, seasoning and bananas and toss well. Dissolve the Mchuzi mix in a little water and pour into the pan. Add the rest of the liquid. Cover and simmer until the bananas are cooked. Serve immediately.

Bananas with Meat

$\frac{1}{4}$ kg cooked meat

12 sliced bananas

4-5 sliced potatoes

Salt

3 tblsp fat

1 large onions, chopped

A few tomatoes, chopped

2 c water

Method:

Wash and cut the meat. Boil it with salt until soft. Peel the bananas, potatoes and onions. Heat the fat and fry the onions until soft. Add into the pan the potatoes, the bananas and the meat. With a little water and seasoning, cook until soft. Mash partially and serve with green vegetables.

Bananas with Tripe

$\frac{1}{2}$ kg tripe

Salt

12 cooking bananas

2 sliced onions

$\frac{1}{2}$ kg sliced tomato

1 tsp tumeric

2 c thin coconut milk

1 c thick coconut milk

Method:

Clean and cut the tripe and cook in salted water until soft and dry. Peel the bananas and cut them into small pieces. Clean and arrange alternate layers of bananas, tripe, sliced onions and tomatoes. Sprinkle the top layer with spices and salt. Add enough thin coconut milk, cover and simmer until the bananas are cooked and most of the liquid is absorbed. Boil the thick coconut milk and pour over the bananas. Serve immediately.

Beef Stew with Rice Rings

$\frac{1}{2}$ kg meat

1 tblsp fat

1 chopped onion

2 cloves of garlic (crushed)

2 tsp curry powder

1 tblsp tomato paste

Salt, pepper

2c water or stock

1 tblsp lemon juice

1 tblsp cornflour

2 c rice

$\frac{1}{2}$ c cooked peas

$\frac{1}{2}$ c carrots (diced and cooked)

Method:

Clean and cut the meat into cubes. Heat the fat and brown the meat. Fry the onion and garlic until cooked. Add in the curry powder, tomato paste, salt and pepper.

Pour in the water, cover and simmer until the meat is cooked. Add the lemon juice and cornflour mixed with a little cold water, stir and heat through.

Boil the rice until cooked and dry. Mix with the peas and carrots. Press into a greased ring mould. Turn out onto a warm serving plate. Serve with the beef stew garnish.

Beef in Beer

1 kg beef

2 tblsp flour

Salt, pepper

50g fat

8 small onions

$\frac{1}{2}$ lt beer

1 tsp vinegar

Parsley

1 bay leaf

2 cloves

2 pepper corns

The parsley, bay leaf, cloves and pepper corns should be tied together.

Placing a layer of meat over onions

Method:

Cut the meat into cubes and toss into seasoned flour. Melt the fat and fry the meat until brown on all sides. Keep aside. Slice 2 onions, toss into the flour and fry in hot oil until soft. Arrange the onions at the base of a casserole, place a layer of meat on them, followed by the rest of the onions and the meat. Top up with small whole peeled onions. Pour beer over the beef, sprinkle with the vinegar and tuck in the tied ingredients. Cook at 325°F for $2\frac{1}{2}$ to 3 hours. Remove the tied ingredients and serve the beef with mashed potatoes and cooked vegetables.

Beef and Cheese Delight

$2\frac{1}{2}$ cups maizemeal flour

4 cups water

Salt

25g margarine

1 chopped onion

$\frac{1}{4}$ kilo minced beef

$\frac{1}{2}$ cup cheddar cheese (grated)

Salt and pepper

2 tomatoes

Method:

Boil the water with a good pinch of salt. Stir in the maizemeal flour and continue stirring until it is cooked. Keep it warm.

Heat the fat in a saucepan and fry the onion until soft. Put in the meat and brown it well. Add it to the cooked maizemeal and cheese and mix well. Heap it in a heat proof dish, place tomato slices on top and sprinkle it with the remaining cheese. Place it under a hot grill to give it a nice brown colour.

Beef Cheese Slice

4 beef slices

1 egg

1 cup fresh breadcrumbs

Salt, pepper

2 tablespoons margarine

50g cheese

Lemon

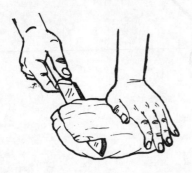

Trimming the meat

Turning the meat over to fry the other side

Method:

Trim the meat, if necessary. Flatten with a rolling pin and dip into the beaten egg before tossing into breadcrumbs mixed with cheese, salt and pepper. Heat the margarine and fry the meat on both sides until cooked and well browned. Arrange in a serving dish and keep warm. Heat the extra fat to a light brown colour and pour over the meat. Garnish with a quartered lemon and serve with vegetables and potatoes.

Beef and Noodle Casserole

2 chopped onions

25g fat

$\frac{1}{2}$ kilo minced meat

Salt, pepper

200g egg noodles, cooked

$\frac{1}{2}$ lt cream of tomato soup

50g grated cheese

Method:

Heat the fat and fry the onions until brown. Add the meat and brown it well. Place the meat, seasoning, noodles and soup in a casserole. Top with the cheese. Bake at 350°F for 30 minutes.

Beef Rolls in Tomatoes

$\frac{1}{2}$ kg beef steak

2 small onions

4 tblsp fat

1 c soft breadcrumbs

2 tblsp parsley

Salt, pepper

$\frac{1}{4}$ kg tomatoes

1 c peas

1 c tomato juice

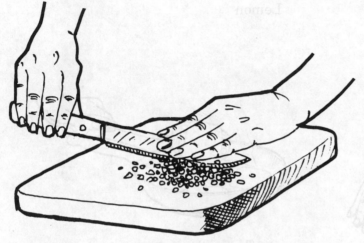

Chopping the onions finely

Method:

Cut the beef into thin slices. Chop the onions finely and mix with 1 tblsp fat, breadcrumbs, chopped parsley and seasoning. Spread the mixture on the slices of meat, roll them up and tie them firmly with a cotton string. Dip the rolls in flour, heat the fat and fry them until brown. Keep them in a casserole. In the same pan, fry the remaining flour for a while before adding the tomatoes, peas, tomato juice and seasoning. Pour this mixture on the beef rolls, cover the casserole and bake at 325°F for about 1 hour, or until the meat is tender. Serve with potatoes or noodles.

Beef Soup

1 kg beef with bones

Salt

4 stalks of chopped celery

$\frac{1}{2}$ kg of chopped carrots

2 large chopped onions

A few cloves and peppercorns

1 bunch of parsley

water

Method:

Cut the beef into pieces and place it in a large pan with water and salt. Boil gently for 1 hour and remove the scum from the surface. Add the chopped vegetables, parsley, crushed cloves and peppercorns. Simmer gently for 1 hour, or until the vegetables are tender. Strain the soup and serve hot with bread.

Beef Stew (Pressure cooked)

$\frac{1}{2}$ kg meat cut into cubes	2 potatoes (diced)
1 tblsp fat	2 carrots (sliced)
Salt, pepper	2 sliced onions
1 cup water	1 cup of peas

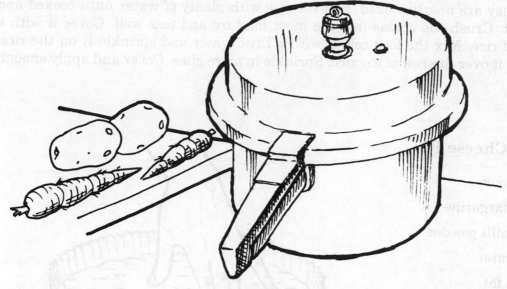

A pressure cooker

Method:

Heat the fat in a pan until hot and brown the meat and onions. Add the salt, pepper and water. Cover and cook for 15 minutes at 15 pound pressure. Cool the pan immediately. Add the diced vegetables, mix well and cook for 5 minutes at 15 pound pressure. Serve with rice.

Biriani

1 kg meat	2 chillies
1 green pawpaw	1 tblsp paprika, pepper
5-8 cloves	$\frac{1}{2}$ lt sour milk
10 cardamons	$\frac{1}{2}$ kg tomatoes
6 sticks cinnamon	1 medium sized tin of tomato paste
2 tsp. crushed garlic	Salt
2 Tblsp. cumin seeds	$\frac{1}{2}$ kg onions
5-8 peppercorns	Yellow food colour
1 bunch dania	2 c fat or oil or ghee
1 tsp. fresh ginger, pounded	1 kg rice

Method:

Grate the pawpaw and cut the meat into pieces. Pound the cloves, cardamons, cinnamon, garlic, jeera, dania, ginger, peppercorns and chillies together. Mix them with the meat, pawpaw, yoghurt, tomatoes, paprika, tomato puree and salt. Marinate for a few hours. Heat the fat and fry the onions till brown and crisp. Remove them from the fat and keep aside. Heat the remaining ghee and fry the meat mixture, simmering until the meat is nearly done. Add the potatoes and continue cooking until they are nearly cooked. Boil the rice with plenty of water until cooked and drain it. Crush the onions into the meat mixture and toss well. Cover it with a layer of rice. Mix the food colour with a little water and sprinkle it on the rice. Spread it over the rest of the rice. Sprinkle in more ghee. Cover and apply enough heat.

Meat Cheese Pie

150g flour

100g margarine

Salt, chilli powder

Cold water

1 tblsp fat

2 onions, sliced

$\frac{1}{2}$ kg cooked meat or chicken

2 eggs

125ml milk

75g grated cheese

Lining a flan tin

Method:

Prepare the pastry and line a flan tin. Heat the fat and fry the onions and meat until brown. Remove from the fire and keep aside. Beat together the eggs, milk and seasoning and most of the cheese. Fill a pastry case with meat and pour the beaten mixture over it. Sprinkle the top with the remaining cheese. Bake at 350°F for 35 to 40 minutes.

Cold Beef

2 tblsp oil

1 large onion

$\frac{1}{4}$ kg diced carrots

$\frac{1}{4}$ kg diced turnips

2 cups water

Salt, pepper

1 tsp paprika
3 bay leaves
1 tsp caraway seeds
1 kg steak

1 tblsp sugar
125ml sour cream
Parsley for garnishing

Method:

Heat the oil and fry the onion until brown. Add the diced carrots and turnips and fry until soft, then 1 cup of water, salt, pepper, paprika, bay leaves and caraway seeds. Finally, add the whole piece of meat or cut it in two. Cook for 2 hours or until cooked. Leave the meat in the sauce until it becomes cold. Drain and strain the sauce. Keep the meat in a fridge for one to two days. Mix the sauce with sugar, 3 tblsp of water and reheat it. Pour in the sour cream and garnish it with parsley. Serve with potatoes, salad and the cold meat cut into slices.

Corned Beef Cakes

200g canned corned beef
25g raw chopped onion
Pepper and salt
200g cooked mashed potatoes

Flour
1 egg
1 c dry breadcrumbs
Oil for frying

Method:

Mix all the ingredients together and shape into cakes. Roll them in flour and dip them in the beaten egg and breadcrumbs. Fry in hot shallow oil. Serve with tomato sauce.

Cutlets

$\frac{1}{2}$ kg minced beef

1 kg potatoes
1 tblsp pilau mixture pounded together
2 onions
2 - 3 cloves of garlic (crushed)

2 - 3 eggs

Salt
Oil for frying
Lemon wedges

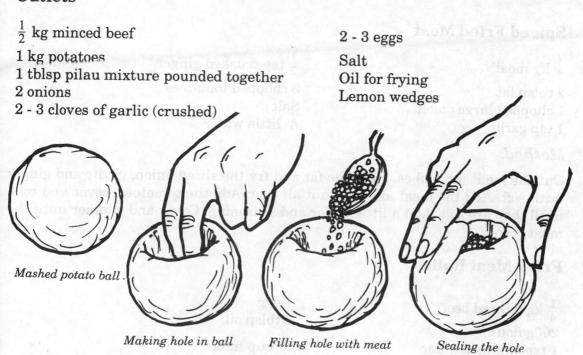

Mashed potato ball   Making hole in ball   Filling hole with meat   Sealing the hole

81

Method:

Peel, cook and mash the potatoes. Grind the garlic and chop the onions. Cook the meat with onions, garlic, pilau mixture and salt until cooked. Shape the mashed potatoes into balls, make a hole in the centre of each and fill it with the meat. Seal the holes. Coat them with beaten eggs and fry in hot oil until well browned. Drain on soft paper and serve with lemon wedges.

Dried Meat Stew

1 kg steak

1 tblsp fat

1 onion

1 chopped sweet pepper

4 chopped tomatoes

1 tsp curry powder

$\frac{1}{4}$ kg potatoes

Salt

$1\frac{1}{2}$ c thin coconut milk

1 c thick coconut milk

Juice of 1 lemon

Method:

Cut the meat into thin strips, salt them well and dry them in the sun or under a very low grill fire. Heat the fat and fry the onion until soft. Add the pepper, tomatoes, curry powder and cook for a few minutes. Add the meat, potatoes, seasoning and the thin coconut milk. Cook until potatoes and meat are tender. Pour in the lemon juice and the thick coconut milk. Lift the stew constantly until the coconut milk is cooked. This prevents the stew from curdling. Serve immediately.

Spiced Fried Meat

$\frac{1}{2}$ kg meat

2 tblsp fat

1 chopped large onion

1 tsp garlic

$\frac{1}{2}$ tsp crushed ginger

3 chopped tomatoes

Salt

A little water

Method:

Cut the meat into cubes. Heat the fat and fry the sliced onion, garlic and ginger until soft. Add the meat and brown it all over. Add the tomatoes, cover and cook until they are soft. Add a little water and seasoning. Cover and simmer until the meat is soft.

Fried Meat Rolls

$\frac{1}{4}$ kg minced beef

200g flour

1 tsp baking powder

1 egg

2 tblsp oil

$\frac{1}{2}$ cup milk

82

1 tblsp chopped parsley

$\frac{1}{2}$ tsp crushed ginger

$\frac{1}{2}$ tsp garam masala

2 cloves of garlic

Salt, pepper

Oil for frying

1 egg

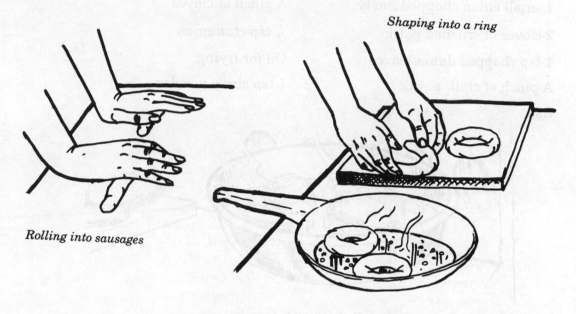

Shaping into a ring

Rolling into sausages

Frying the ring in hot oil

Method:

Mix all the ingredients together, except the oil and the egg, and knead with milk. Take a small portion of the mixture and roll into a sausage. Shape it into a ring and fry in hot oil. Cool it, dip in the beaten egg and fry again.

Fried Mutton

$\frac{1}{2}$ kg mutton

2 onions

$\frac{1}{4}$ kg tomatoes

Salt

Fat

Method:

Heat the fat and fry the onions until soft. Add the tomatoes and meat, season and cook in a covered pan until meat is tender.

Kebabs

$\frac{1}{4}$ kg minced beef

1 slice of bread soaked in water

1 small onion chopped finely

2 cloves of crushed garlic

1 tsp chopped dania leaves

A pinch of chilli powder

Salt

1 tsp chopped ginger

1 chilli

A pinch of cloves

$\frac{1}{2}$ tsp cinnamon

Oil for frying

1 tsp curry powder

Frying the kebabs

Method:

Mix all the dry ingredients, except the oil. Add the minced meat, onion, garlic and dania. Squeeze out the liquid from the bread. Mix the bread with the other ingredients. Shape the mixture into balls or logs and fry in hot oil until cooked. Serve with tea or any other drink, or with curry sauce and plain rice.

Liver and Potato Casserole

$\frac{1}{2}$ kg liver

2 tblsp flour

Salt, pepper

2 tblsp fat

1 kg sliced potataoes

3-4 large onions, sliced

$\frac{1}{2}$ lt white sauce

A few slices of tomatoes

$\frac{1}{2}$ cup grated cheese

Layering cutting the casserole

Method:

Slice the liver and remove the skin and veins. Toss it into seasoned flour. Heat the fat and fry the liver for 5 minutes. Remove it from the pan and keep aside. Slice the onions and fry until soft. Add the potatoes and toss well. Arrange the food in layers in a casserole, starting with the liver, followed by the onions, the potatoes and the last layer consisting of onions. Add the white sauce and arrange the slices of tomatoes. Bake at 375°F for 25 to 30 minutes, or until the potatoes are cooked. Sprinkle the top with cheese.

Lunchtime Meat Loaf

1 kg.minced beef	1 tblsp chopped parsley
50g fresh breadcrumbs	Salt, pepper
1 chopped onion	1 hard boiled egg
2 large eggs	25g grated cheddar cheese

Method:

Mix the first six ingredients together and fill a 2 lb loaf tin with half of the mixture. Chop the boiled egg, mix it with the grated cheese and spread it over the mixture. Top up with the remaining mixture. Cover with foil paper and bake for $1\frac{3}{4}$ hours at 350°F. Loosen the sides and turn it onto a platter. Serve with potatoes, vegetable salad and tomato sauce.

Marinated Steak

4 slices of beef steak	2 chillies
2 chopped onions	1 cup of cooked corn
1 piece of ginger	A pinch of saffron
2 tsp lemon juice	A pinch of sugar
$\frac{1}{2}$ cup thick coconut milk	Salt
1 large sliced green pepper	

Method:

Trim off the fat from the meat. Pound the chillies, onion and ginger and moisten with lemon juice. To the coconut milk add salt, sugar and saffron. Mix well. Pour over the steaks and marinate for $2\frac{1}{2}$ hours, turning them over from time to time. Grill the steak until cooked.

Cook the corn in coconut milk. Arrange the steaks on a platter and pour the corn over them. Garnish with sliced pepper.

Marinated Steak Cocktail

3 tblsp soy sauce

3 tblsp lemon juice

Salt, pepper

1 tsp ginger

$\frac{1}{2}$ kg steak

2 tblsp cornflour

Oil for frying

2 sliced onions

1 sweet green pepper (chopped)

2 chopped tomatoes

Chilli sauce

1 cup water

Method:

Cut the steak into 1" cubes. Blend the soy sauce, lemon juice, ginger, salt and pepper. Marinate the steak in this mixture for one hour. Remove them, toss them into cornflour and fry them in hot oil until cooked. Drain and keep aside. Heat 2 tblsp of oil and fry the onions until soft. Add the pepper and tomatoes and cook until soft, then the seasoning, water, chilli sauce and the marinade. Bring to boil. Thicken, if necessary, with left over cornflour.

Serve the meat on cocktail sticks to be dipped in sauce as it is eaten.

Meatballs with Vegetables

$\frac{1}{2}$ kg minced beef

1 cup breadcrumbs

1 egg

Salt, pepper

1 cup cooked carrots

2 green sweet pepper (diced)

1 cup cooked peas

A little oil

2 teaspoons cornflour

1 cup stock or water

Method:

Combine the meat with breadcrumbs, egg and seasoning. Shape into balls and fry in hot oil until brown. Add the peas, carrots, pepper, enough stock and seasoning. Cover and cook for 15 minutes. Thicken with cornflour and serve with noodles or rice.

Meat and Corn Dish

$\frac{1}{2}$ kg cooked steak, minced or cubed

1 finely chopped onion

$\frac{1}{2}$ c cooked beans

1 tomato

Salt, pepper

2 eggs

2 tablespoons milk

Topping:

1 small can of corn

1 small onion

50g breadcrumbs

A knob of butter

Method:

Mix the meat, onion, beans and chopped tomato and season well. Bind with beaten eggs and milk and pour into a greased casserole.

Spreading corn and onion over the meat

Topping:

Mix the corn and chopped onion and spread over the meat. Sprinkle with breadcrumbs and dot with butter. Bake at 350°F for 30 to 40 minutes, or until the meat is cooked.

Meat Loaf

1 cup soft breadcrumbs	1 small onion, grated
1 kg minced beef	2 finely chopped carrots
2 eggs	Chopped parsley
Salt, pepper	Milk

Method:

Mix all the ingredients well. Press the mixture into a greased and lined 9" x 5" loaf tin. Bake at 350°F for $1\frac{1}{2}$ hours, or until cooked. Garnish with parsley and slices of tomatoes and serve with potatoes.

Meat Filled Pancakes

$\frac{1}{4}$ kilo minced meat

1 onion

Tomato sauce

Salt, pepper,

1 tomato

1 tblsp chopped dania

Chopped green chillies

1 oz fat

Tomato sauce

For the batter you need:

$\frac{1}{2}$ pt pancake batter

150gm flour

2 eggs

Salt

Water

Oil for frying

Filling pancake with meat

Rolling up the pancake

Method:

Peel and chop the onion, tomato, chillies and dania. Heat the fat and fry the onion and meat until brown. Add the dania, tomato, chillies, salt and pepper. Cook until the liquid dries out. Keep aside.

Sieve the flour and salt into a container. Add the eggs and enough water to make a running consistency or batter. Heat the oil and cook the pancakes. Fill the pancakes with the meat and roll them up. Garnish with tomatoes and parsley and serve with tomato sauce.

Meat Stew

$\frac{1}{2}$ kg steak	1 cup peas
2 onions	1 cup diced carrots
2 tomatoes	4 medium diced potatoes
1 small piece of ginger	Salt, pepper
3 cloves of garlic	2 cups water
1 tsp curry powder	

Method:

Cut the meat into cubes and slice the onions and tomatoes. Crush the garlic and ginger. Heat the oil and fry the onion until soft. Add the garlic, ginger, tomatoes and curry powder and cook for a while before browning the meat in it. Add the peas and carrots, seasoning and enough water. Cook until the meat is tender, add the diced potatoes and cook for 15 minutes.

Meat with Scones Topping

2 tblsp fat

2 onions

2 cloves of garlic

$\frac{1}{2}$ kg minced meat

1 tsp curry powder

1 sweet pepper

1 cup tomatoes

Salt

$\frac{1}{2}$ cup water

Topping:

100g flour

50g maizemeal

$1\frac{1}{2}$ tsp baking powder

2 tblsp margarine

Salt

A little milk

An egg for brushing

Method:

Cut the meat into cubes, peel and slice the onions, dice the pepper, peel and chop tomatoes. Heat the fat and fry the onions, garlic and meat until brown. Add the curry powder, pepper and tomatoes. Cook for a while before putting in the remaining ingredients. Transfer to a casserole, cover and bake for 2 hours at 300°F.

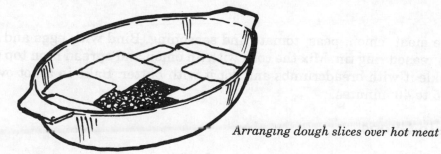

Arranging dough slices over hot meat

Topping:

Sift the flour together with baking powder and salt. Rub in the fat and bind with milk to form a soft dough. Cut into neat shapes and arrange on top of the hot meat. Brush the top with milk or egg. Bake at 425°F for 15 to 20 minutes, or until the top is well browned. Serve with a salad or vegetables.

Meat Balls in a Nest

$\frac{1}{2}$ kg minced beef

1 chopped onion

1 - 2 eggs

100g breadcrumbs

Salt, pepper

1 cup of oil

$1\frac{1}{2}$ cups cream of tomato soup

1 onion

2 tblsp chopped sweet pepper

Cooked potatoes or spaghetti

Method:

Mix the meat, onion, egg, breadcrumbs, salt and pepper. Shape the mixture into small balls. Fry in hot oil until well browned. Remove them from the pan and keep them aside. Reduce the oil in the pan to 2 tblsp and fry the onion and pepper. Pour the tomato soup into the pan and put the meatballs in it. Cook until it thickens. Arrange the potatoes into a nest shape and fill the centre with meatballs.

Meat Ring with Corn

$\frac{1}{2}$ kg minced beef

1 chopped onion

$\frac{1}{2}$ cup cooked peas

1 tomato, skinned and chopped

Salt, pepper

2 eggs

2 tblsp milk

Topping:

2 cups cooked corn

1 chopped onion

50g breadcrumbs

Butter

Method:

Combine the meat, onion, peas, tomato and seasoning. Bind with eggs and milk. Pour into a greased ring tin. Mix the corn with an onion and spread it on top of the meat. Sprinkle it with breadcrumbs and dot it with butter. Bake in a hot oven at 350°F for 35 to 40 minutes.

Meat Potato Chops

$\frac{1}{2}$ kg minced beef

5 - 6 medium potatoes (boiled)

Salt

1 tsp garlic and ginger, crushed

1 tsp garam masala

3 grated onions

1 bunch of dania

1 tsp crushed green chillies

1 egg

Oil for frying

Lettuce

Method:

Place the meat in a pan with onions, garlic, ginger, salt, chillies and garam masala. Cook until all the liquid dries up. Peel and mash the potatoes. Mix them with the meat, shape into balls and press into patties. Beat the egg, dip the chops in it and fry in hot oil until brown and crisp on both sides. Be careful not to turn them over too soon or they will break. Serve on a bed of lettuce with tomato sauce.

Minced Beef and Peas Pie

1 kg minced beef
1 cup of cooked carrots, diced
1 cup peas, cooked
2 tblsp fat
1 onion, chopped
2 tblsp chopped parsely
or 1 tsp mixed herbs
1 cup of water or stock
Seasoning (salt and pepper)
1 tblsp flour
Mashed potatoes
1 tblsp butter
A little milk
1 egg

Spreading mashed potatoes over meat

Method:

Heat the fat and fry the onion and meat until brown. Add the carrots, peas, parsley, herbs, stock and seasoning and simmer for a few minutes. Add the flour to thicken and pour into a deep pie or casserole dish. Heat the mashed potatoes and mix in the butter and milk. Spoon and spread them over the meat and brush with a beaten egg. Bake at 375°F for 40 to 45 minutes or until brown, or place under a hot grill.

Minced Meat Pinwheels

Scone Dough:
200g flour
3 tsp baking powder
1 tsp salt
50g margarine
Water for mixing

Filling:
1 small onion
2 tblsp fat
$\frac{1}{2}$ kg minced meat
Salt, pepper
3 tblsp tomato sauce

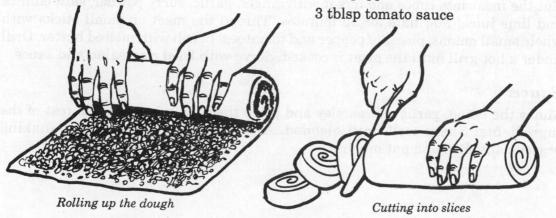

Rolling up the dough   *Cutting into slices*

Method:

Filling

Heat the fat and fry the onion until brown before adding the meat and browning it. Season with salt, pepper and sauce. Allow to cool.

Scone Dough

Sift together the flour, salt and baking powder. Rub in the margarine and bind with water. Roll it out into a rectangle of about 1/4 inch in thickness. Spread the filling on it. Roll it up like a swiss roll. Cut into 1 inch thick slices. Bake on ungreased baking trays at 450°F for 15 minutes. Garnish with parsley and serve with tomato sauce.

Mishkaki

$\frac{1}{2}$ kg steak

1 tsp crushed ginger

3 cloves of garlic, crushed

$\frac{1}{2}$ tsp curry powder

2 chillies

Juice of 1 lime

Salt

Butter (melted)

Small onions

2 sweet peppers

4 tomatoes

Sauce:

$\frac{1}{2}$ onion

1 clove of garlic

2 tblsp butter

1 bunch of crushed parsley or dania

2 tblsp vinegar

$\frac{1}{2}$ cup tomato sauce

Salt, pepper

$\frac{1}{4}$ cup water

Method:

Cut the meat into cubes and mix it with ginger, garlic, curry powder, salt, chillies and lime juice. Marinate for 30 minutes. Thread the meat on small sticks with whole small onions, pieces of pepper and tomatoes. Brush with melted butter. Grill under a hot grill until the meat is cooked. Serve with fried rice, salad and sauce.

Sauce:

Mince the onion, garlic and parsley and place them in a jar with the rest of the ingredients. Shake well until blended. Allow to stand for 24 hours, shaking ocassionally. Boil and put into use.

Mutton Curry

1 kg mutton	1 tsp fresh ginger, pounded
4 tblsp oil	3-4 cloves of garlic
2 large onions, sliced	2 tblsp tomato paste
1 tsp cumin seeds	6 chopped tomatoes
$\frac{1}{2}$ tsp cinnamon powder	Salt
$\frac{1}{2}$ tsp cloves, powdered	$\frac{1}{2}$ cup water
1 tsp tumeric	

Method:

Cut the meat into pieces. Fry the onions and garlic until brown. Add the other ingredients and the meat and cook slowly until the liquid dries out. Pour in the water and simmer until the meat is cooked and the gravy is thick. Serve with Chutney and curry accompaniments like diced ripe bananas, grated coconut, chopped onions and tomatoes, pineapple cubes, etc.

Nyama Choma

1 kg mutton

Salt

Pepper

Lemon juice

2 tblsp fat

A grill for roasting meat

Method:

Heat up the grill and place the meat under it. Sprinkle salt, pepper and lemon juice on the meat while under the hot grill. Baste it with fat on both sides and a little salt. Cook until done. Serve with Kachumbari.

Oxtail Stew

1 oxtail	1 c chopped tomatoes
2 tblsp flour	1 cup diced carrots
Salt, paprika	1 cup peas
A little fat	Water
2 sliced onions	Boiled potatoes

Method:

Clean and cut the oxtail at the joints and toss into seasoned flour. Heat the fat and brown the pieces on all sides. Remove them from the pan and keep aside. In the same pan, fry the onions until golden brown. Add the tomatoes and cook until soft. Return the oxtail into the pan and add enough liquid. Simmer for 1 - 1$\frac{1}{2}$ hours, or until the meat is almost tender. Add the peas and the carrots and cook until the peas are done. Serve with rice.

Grilled Marinated Mutton

1 kg mutton
1 head of garlic, crushed
1 small piece of crushed ginger

Juice of 2 lemons
Salt, masala
A little oil

Method:

Clean and wipe dry the mutton. Cut into flat chunks. Marinate them in a mixture of the remaining ingredients, except the oil, for about 1 hour. Heat up a grill and place the meat on a rack. Roast on medium heat and brush with oil from time to time until the meat is cooked on both sides. Serve with Kachumbari.

You may also cut meat into smaller pieces. After marinating, arrange on a skewer and roast or grill or cook in a pan.

Samosas

200g plain flour
$\frac{1}{2}$ tsp salt
A little oil and flour
125ml warm water

Filling:

$\frac{1}{2}$ kg minced beef
$\frac{1}{2}$ tsp crushed fresh ginger
Salt
$\frac{1}{4}$ tsp cinnamon powder
2 tblsp chopped green dania
1 clove of crushed garlic
1-2 green chillies, seeded and chopped.
$\frac{1}{4}$ tsp powdered cloves
$\frac{1}{2}$ cup chopped onion

Paste:

2 tblsp plain flour
3-4 tblsp warm water
Oil for frying
Lemon wedges

Rolling out the dough

Spreading oil on dough

Drying in a frying pan

Method:

Sift the flour and salt and bind with water. Knead the dough well on a floured board. Take walnut size balls of dough and roll out into circular shapes of about 8cm in diameter. Brush each piece with oil and dust with flour. Sandwich two pieces together, sealing in the oil and flour. Roll them out again, as thin as possible, between 22 and 24cm in diameter. Dry both sides of the pastry on a hot frying pan. Separate the layers and keep them in a damp tea towel. Treat the rest of the dough in the same way. Now cut each piece into three. Each section will make one samosa. Fold the pastry and fill it with about 1 dessert spoonful of the filling. Seal the ends with paste. Fry in hot oil until golden brown and drain on absorbent paper. Serve hot with lemon wedges.

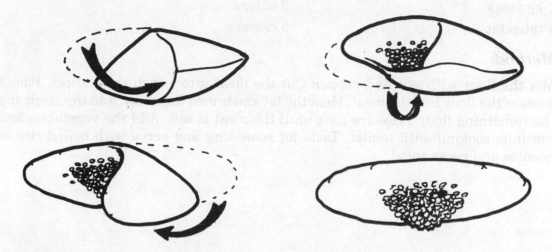

Filling:

Wash the minced beef and cook until well browned. Add garlic, ginger, chillies, salt, cinnamon and cloves and simmer for a few minutes. Remove from the heat and stir in the onions and dania. Cool and use as above.

Paste:

Mix flour and water to make a sticky paste. Use it to seal the samosa ends together.

Skillet Dinner

1 tblsp fat	2 tblsp tomato puree
$\frac{1}{2}$ kg minced beef	$2\frac{1}{4}$ cups water
1 chopped onion	A pinch of sugar
$\frac{1}{2}$ tsp crushed garlic	80g noodles or spaghetti
2 tblsp chopped parsley	Grated carrots
Salt, pepper	

Method:

Heat the fat in a heavy pan and slightly brown the meat, onion, garlic and parsley. Mix the tomato puree with water, sugar and pepper until smooth. Add to the meat and mix well. Cover and simmer for 10 minutes. Add the noodles and cook until ready, stirring ocassionally. Serve sprinkled with grated cheese.

Steak in Gravy

2 tblsp flour
Salt and pepper
1 kg steak
3 tblsp fat

1-2 cups stock
2 sweet peppers
2 onions
5 carrots

Method:

Mix the flour with salt and pepper. Cut the meat into 1 inch thick slices. Pound some of the flour into the meat. Heat the fat and brown the meat. Add the stock and the remaining flour. Pressure cook until the meat is soft. Add the vegetables and continue cooking until tender. Taste for seasoning and serve with boiled rice or noodles and green salad.

Puddings

Types of Pudding

Apple Ring

Banana Jelly Pudding

Boiled Fruit Pudding

Bokoboko Bananas

Chocolate Pudding

Choux Buns Pyramid

Coconut Pudding

Coconut Sweet Potato Pudding

Crumbs and Raisins Pudding

Fruit Basket

Fruit Scramble

Fruit Salad Savarin

Ginger Pudding

Halwa

Lemon Curd

Lemon Coconut Pudding

Melon Basket

Marmalade Pudding

Milky Rice Pudding

Nut Toffees

Pawpaw Pie

Pineapple Custard Pudding

Pineapple Pancakes

Pudding Butterscotch

Pineapple Pie

Scrambled Bread Pudding

Semolina Mould

Swiss Roll Sweet

Toffee Potatoes

Apple Rings

175g flour	$\frac{1}{4}$ pt milk
2 tsp baking powder	Apples cut into slices
25g cornflour	Cream
25g sugar	Extra milk for brushing
25g margarine	A little sugar for dredging

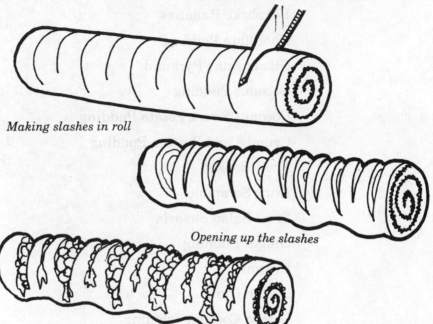

Making slashes in roll

Opening up the slashes

With fruit and cream filling

Method:

Sift together the flour, cornflour and baking powder. Rub in the margarine and add the sugar. Bind with milk to form a soft dough. Knead roughly and roll it out into an oblong. Dampen the edges and roll it up like a swiss roll. Place on a baking tray and shape into a ring. Make 10 slashes across the roll and twist each slash a little to its side. Brush with milk and dredge with sugar. Bake at 450°F for 15 to 20 minutes. Allow to cool and fill the centre and the slashes with fruit and cream.

Banana Jelly Pudding

250ml water	6 ripe bananas, mashed
1 pkt of Jelly crystals	Sugar to taste
3 eggs (separated)	

Method:

Heat the water add it to the Jelly and stir until the jelly dissolves. Beat the egg yolks with sugar until they thicken and add to the mashed bananas and cooled jelly. Beat the egg whites until stiff and fold into the banana mixture. Pour into a mould and put into a fridge to set. Serve decorated with cream.

Boiled Fruit Pudding

75g margarine

75g sugar

2 eggs

100g self raising flour

100g mixed fruit

A little milk

Preparing to cook in boiling water

Method:

Cream the margarine and sugar until fluffy. Stir in the eggs, sifted flour, fruits and a little milk to make a dropping consistency. Pour into a greased 1 lt. pudding basin. Cover and cook in boiling water for $1\frac{1}{2}$ hours. Serve hot with any sweet sauce or hot butter sauce.

Bokoboko Bananas

5 - 6 ripe Bokoboko bananas

Some thick coconut milk

Some thin coconut milk

A good pinch of sugar

A few cardamons

Pouring the coconut milk over bananas

Method:

Peel and slice the bananas and arrange them in a pan. Sprinkle them with sugar and ground cardamons. Pour in enough thin coconut milk. Cook covered until the bananas are tender and the liquid is almost absorbed. Boil the thick coconut milk separately to make it thicker. Pour over the bananas and serve.

Bokoboko bananas are short fat bananas mainly found at the Kenyan Coast.

Chocolate Pudding

1 tblsp cocoa	250ml milk
$\frac{1}{2}$ tblsp sugar	Butter
$1\frac{1}{2}$ tblsp cornflour	Vanilla essence

Method:

Mix the cocoa, sugar and cold milk into a paste. Boil the rest of the milk and pour into the paste. Return to the fire and bring to boil, stirring constantly until it thickens. Add the vanilla and a knob of butter. Pour into a mould and allow to set.

Choux Buns Pyramid

Pastry:

	Sauce:
50g butter	50g butter
125ml water	1 tbs sugar syrup or honey
Pinch of salt	2 tblsp cocoa
2 eggs	125ml water

Filling:

125ml cream

25g sugar

Method:

Heat the water, butter and salt until the butter melts. Sift the flour into the water and butter. Beat it with a wooden spoon until the mixture forms into a ball and detaches from the sides of the pan. Cool it slightly. Beat in the eggs, one at a time, until the mixture becomes smooth. Place it in a piping bag and squeeze mounds onto a greased baking tray, or use a spoon. Bake at 425°F for 10 minutes. Reduce the heat to 350°F and bake for a further 15 minutes. Cool them. Slit along the sides and fill with the cream beaten together with sugar until thick.

Melt the butter and syrup together, add the cocoa and cook for 2 to 3 minutes, stirring to prevent it from sticking. Add the water and bring to boil, stirring until smooth. Cool slightly. Pile the buns in a serving dish and pour the sauce over them.

Coconut Pudding

100g fresh breadcrumbs	25g butter
100g grated desiccated coconut	100g sugar
$\frac{1}{2}$ litre hot milk	$\frac{1}{2}$ grated rind of lemon
1 egg	50g jam

Method:

Mix the crumbs with milk, coconut, butter, sugar, egg and grated rind. Grease a baking pudding dish with butter. Spread the jam at the bottom and pour the mixture over it. Bake at 350°F for 30 minutes.

Coconut Sweet Potato Pudding

2 tblsp sugar	$\frac{1}{2}$ cup water
$1\frac{1}{2}$ cups sweet potatoes, cooked and mashed	$\frac{3}{4}$ cup milk
1 cup grated coconut	2 eggs
4 tblsp melted butter	$\frac{1}{2}$ tsp mixed spices

Method:

Mix sugar, potatoes and coconut. Beat in thoroughly the butter, milk and water. Beat in the eggs gradually and add the spices. Beat until smooth, pour into a greased heat proof dish and bake at 350 F for 50 to 60 minutes, or until golden brown. Serve hot.

Crumbs and Raisins Pudding

2 cups milk	$\frac{1}{4}$ cup sugar
$1\frac{1}{2}$ cups soft breadcrumbs	$\frac{1}{2}$ cup raisins
1 tblsp butter	2 eggs

Method:

Heat the milk, pour it into the breadcrumbs and butter and stir until the butter melts. Beat the eggs, sugar, salt and raisins together. Slowly add in the milk mixture. Pour into a greased baking dish and stand it in a pan of hot water. Bake at 350°F for 1 hour, or until it sets. Serve hot with custard or cold with cream.

Fruit Basket

150g sugar

150g eggs

175g flour

25g cocoa

Chocolate butter cream

Mixed fruit

Whipped cream

Chocolate vermicelli

Filling the ring in the cake with fruit and nuts

Method:

Whisk the eggs and sugar until thick. Fold in the sieved flour and cocoa and divide into three sandwich tins. Bake at 350°F for 15 to 20 minutes. Cool it.

Sandwich two cakes together with some of the cream. Coat one side with cream and sprinkle with chocolate vermicelli. Cut a circle out of the third cake and coat with chocolate icing. Place the third cake on top of the others, coating as before. Fill the centre with whipped cream and fruits. Decorate the edges with cream.

Fruit Crumble

2 cups chopped fruit (pears or apple or pineapple)	150g flour
50g sugar	100g margarine
1 tblsp margarine	50g sugar
A little water	1 tblsp icing sugar

Pressing the sugar down over the fruit

Method:

Toss the fruits into the sugar and place them in a heat proof dish. Dot with 1tblsp of margarine. Sift the flour and rub in the margarine. Mix in the sugar and 1 tblsp of water. Spread it over the fruit and press it down. Bake at 350°F for 1 hour or until the crumble is browned. Sprinkle with icing sugar and serve with a pouring of custard or fresh cream.

Fruit Salad Savarin

100g sugar	2 eggs
100g margarine	250g tinned fruit salad. Reserve the liquid
4 tblsp instant coffee	$\frac{1}{2}$ c black coffee
4 tblsp flour	1 carton cream
$\frac{1}{2}$ tsp baking powder	

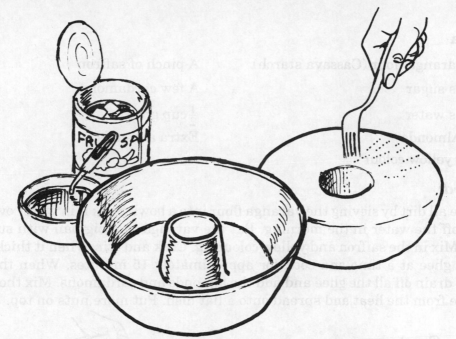

Pricking the cake in preparation for the coffee

Method:

Cream fat and sugar until creamy. Beat in the eggs and sift and fold in the flour and coffee. Pour into a ring tin and bake at 375°F for 20 to 30 minutes. Allow to cool. Mix the juice from the tinned fruit with black coffee. Prick the cake and spoon the mixed liquid over it until it becomes soaked. Fill the centre with the fruit and arrange a few around the cake. Whip the cream and put it in a piping nozzle. Pipe the cake with cream and serve.

Ginger Pudding

2 tblsp flour

1 cup soft breadcrumbs

3 tblsp Kimbo or margarine

$\frac{1}{2}$ tsp baking powder

1 tblsp chopped ginger

2 tblsp golden syrup or honey

$\frac{1}{2}$ to $\frac{3}{4}$ cup milk

1 egg

Steaming in boiling water

Method:

Mix all the dry ingredients together with the syrup, egg and enough milk to make a fairly firm mixture. Put it into a greased bowl, cover with foil paper and tie with a string. Place it in a pan of boiling water. Cover the pan and steam for 1 to $1\frac{1}{2}$ hours, or until firm and cooked. Serve with a sweet pudding sauce.

NB: Boil the ginger in sugar and water until soft. Chop or use tinned cooked ginger in sugar syrup.

Halwa

1 cup varanga flour (Cassava starch)

$2\frac{1}{2}$ cups sugar

$2\frac{1}{2}$ cups water

A few Almonds

A little yellow colour

A pinch of saffron

A few cardamons

$\frac{1}{2}$ cup ghee

Extra almonds

Method:

Remove all dirt by sieving the varanga flour into a bowl. Soak it in water overnight. Drain off the water in the morning. Put the varanga in a big pan with sugar and water. Mix in the saffron and yellow colouring. Cook and stir. When it thickens add a little ghee at a time and cook for approximately 15 minutes. When the halwa shines, drain off all the ghee and add the almonds and cardamons. Mix thoroughly. Remove from the heat and spread onto a flat dish. Put more nuts on top.

Lemon Curd

100g butter

Juice and rind of 4 lemons

$\frac{1}{2}$ kg sugar

4 beaten and strained eggs

Method:

Place the sugar, butter and lemon at the top of a double pan. Simmer and stir until the sugar dissolves. Stir in the eggs until the mixture thickens and is creamy. Strain, cover and store in a cool place for up to one month.

Lemon Coconut Pudding

25g margarine

200g sugar

4 eggs, separated

Juice and rind of 2 lemons

125g desiccated coconut

2 tblsp flour

1 cup milk

1 tsp red jam

Method:

Cream the margarine and the sugar. Beat in the yolks. Blend in the lemon juice and grated rind. Fold in 75gm of the coconut and flour and stir in the milk. Beat the egg whites until stiff and fold into the mixture. Pour into a greased pudding bowl. Place in a baking tray with $\frac{1}{2}$ cup of hot water. Bake on the top rack of the oven at 350°F for $1\frac{1}{2}$ hours. Before serving, toast the remaining coconut and decorate the top with it and a little jam.

Melon Basket

1 water melon

A mixture of fruits

Sugar or $\frac{1}{2}$ cup orange squash

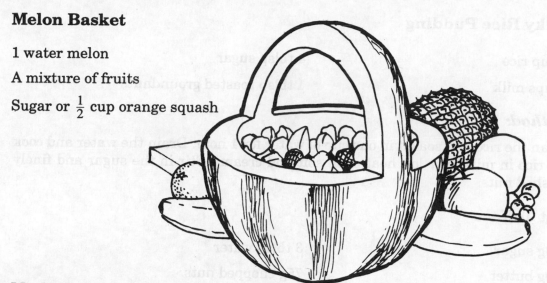

Method:

Clean and shape the melon into a basket with a handle. Scoop out the fruit and chop it into smaller pieces. Clean and cut the other fruits and mix them with the pieces of melon. Sweeten with the sugar and return them into the melon shell. Serve with fresh cream or custard.

Marmalade Pudding

50g flour

1 level teaspoon baking powder

50g soft breadcrumbs

50g fat

50g Sugar

3 tblsp marmalade

1 egg

Sauce:

1-2 tblsp milk

2 level tsp cornflour

125ml water

$\frac{1}{2}$ lemon juice

$\frac{1}{2}$ tbsp marmalade

Sugar

Method:

Sift the flour and baking powder into a bowl. Stir in the bread crumbs, fat and sugar. Add the 2 tblsp marmalade and the slightly mixed egg. Stir the mixture with milk for 30 seconds to produce a dropping consistency.

Grease a pudding basin and put in the remaining marmalade. Turn the mixture into the basin, cover with a grease proof paper and tie. Steam for 2 hours.

Prepare marmalade sauce by blending the cornflour and water in a saucepan. Add the lemon juice and marmalade. Stir over low heat until the mixture thickens. Taste and add a little sugar if necessary. Turn out the pudding onto a plate and serve hot with the marmalade sauce.

Milky Rice Pudding

$\frac{1}{2}$ cup rice

3 cups milk

4 tblsp sugar

1 tblsp roasted groundnuts

Method:

Clean the rice and soak it in one cup of water for 1 hour. Drain the water and cook the rice in milk over low heat until soft and creamy. Stir in the sugar and finely crushed nuts.

Nut Toffees

200g sugar

200g butter

1 tblsp golden syrup

3 tblsp water

75g chopped nuts

Plain chocolate

Method:

Cook the sugar, butter, syrup and water until a hard ball forms when tested by dropping a little into cold water.

Grease a pie plate and sprinkle the chopped nuts in it. Pour the hot syrup over the nuts and sprinkle it with more nuts and chopped chocolate. When cold, crack into pieces and serve.

Pawpaw Pie

2 ripe medium sized pawpaws

1 tblsp lemon juice

$\frac{1}{4}$ tsp cinnamon

$\frac{1}{2}$ cup sugar

1 tsp vanilla essence

A dash of nutmeg

3 tblsp melted butter

150g shortcrust pastry

Mashing the pawpaw through a sieve

Method:

Wash and peel the pawpaw. Dice and cook it in water until soft. Drain off the liquid and mash it through a sieve. Add the sugar, lemon juice, cinnamon, vanilla, nutmeg, and butter. Mix well and pour into an unbaked pie shell. Decorate the top with pastry strips and bake at 400°F until the crust is golden brown.

Pineapple Custard Pudding

1 pineapple

500 ml cooked custard

1 pkt gelatine

A little cold water

Method:

Pouring custard into pineapple shells

Clean and cut the pineapple lengthwise and scoop out the flesh. Prepare the custard and cool it. Dissolve the gelatine in cold water and stir in the custard with a little mashed pineapple pulp. Pour into the half pineapple shell and chill it until it sets. Decorate with pineapple leaves and serve with cream.

Pineapple Pancakes

Batter:

1 tblsp sugar

50g flour

2 eggs

1 tblsp melted butter

$\frac{1}{4}$ pt milk

A little oil

Spooning the pineapples onto the pancake

Filling:

8 tblsp pineapple syrup

50g sugar

3 tblsp butter

1 cup pineapple pieces

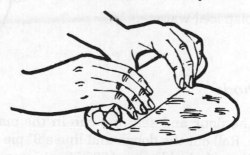

Method:

Rolling up the pancake

Sift the flour and sugar and add the rest of the ingredients for the batter. Beat until smooth. Heat a small amount of oil in a frying pan and pour about 2 tblsp of the batter mixture into it. Cook until brown, turn and cook the other side. Remove from the pan and cover with a clean cloth. Repeat the process until all the mixture is used up.

Boil the syrup, sugar and butter and mix with the chopped pineapple. Use about 1 tblsp to fill up each pancake. Serve the remaining sauce separately.

Pudding Butterscotch

100g sugar

$\frac{1}{2}$ litre milk

$1\frac{1}{2}$ tblsp cornflour

Vanilla essence

1 tblsp butter

Pouring mixture into a pudding bowl

Method:

Cook the sugar in a pan on medium heat until it turns brown. Remove from the heat and pour the milk into the pan, reserving a little for dissolving the cornflour. Return the pan to the fire and heat it until it almost boils. Mix the cornflour with the remaining milk and add to heated milk and sugar. Stir until the mixture boils and thickens. Remove from the heat and add the essence and butter. Pour into a pudding bowl. Allow to cool. Serve with cream, if preferred.

Pineapple Pie

150 g flour

100 g margarine

A pinch of salt

2-3 tblsp iced water

Binding using a knife

Method:

Sift the flour and salt and rub in the margarine. Bind with water using a table knife. Roll out the dough and line a 9" pie dish. Prick the bottom of the dough with a fork and bake blind at 450°F for 15 minutes. Remove the centre paper and bake for a further 5 to 10 minutes. Cool and use as required.

Filling:

1 large tin of pineapple pieces	$\frac{1}{4}$ litre pineapple juice
4 tblsp sugar	1 tblsp margarine
2 tbisp Cornflour	Vanilla essence
2 eggs	Food colour

108

Method:

Drain the pineapple and reserve the juice. In a pan, mix the sugar, cornflour and eggs and stir in the pineapple pieces and 6 tblsp of pineapple juice. Cook on low heat until cooked and thickened. Remove from the heat and stir in the margarine, vanilla and food colour. Cool and fill the pastry with it.

Scrambled Bread Pudding

4 thick slices of stale bread

375ml milk

$\frac{1}{2}$ cup sultanas

1 apple (peeled and chopped)

1 egg

25g sugar

100g butter or oil

Method:

Cut the bread into cubes and put them in a bowl. Mix all the remaining ingredients together, except the butter, and pour onto the bread. Let it soak for about 15 minutes. Heat a little butter in a frying pan and put the bread in it. Fry all sides until brown. Serve with a little sugar flavoured with vanilla.

Semolina Mould

3 tblsp semolina

500 ml milk

Grated rind of 1 orange

50g sugar

2 eggs

1 c canned fruits

Method:

Blend the semolina with a little cold milk. Heat the remaining milk with the orange rind and sugar. Add the semolina and stir until the mixture boils. Remove it from the heat and cool slightly. Beat in the eggs thoroughly. Pour into a rinsed mould and keep it in a cool place. When firm and set, turn out onto a serving plate and decorate with fruits. Serve immediately.

Swiss Roll Sweet

1 Swiss roll

1 cup mixed fresh fruits

1c fruit juice

2 tablespoons custard powder

500 ml milk

2-3 tablespoons sugar

Vanilla essence

Method:

Cut the Swiss roll into slices and arrange them in the base and sides of a pudding bowl. Moisten them with the fruit juice and spread the mixed fruits on them.

Mix a little cold milk with the sugar and custard powder. Heat the remaining milk and pour the custard in it. Stir until the mixture boils and is smooth and thick. Add the vanilla, cool it a little and pour over the fruits. Let the mixture cool before chilling it in the fridge. Serve with cream, angelica and fruits.

Toffee Potatoes

Syrup:

25g sugar	75g flour
2 tblsp honey or golden syrup	2 tsp sugar
125ml water	2 eggs, separated
Juice of 1 lemon	375 ml water
4 large potatoes	Oil for frying

Method:

Boil the sugar, honey, water and lemon juice. Peel the potatoes, cut them into thick segments, put them into hot syrup and parboil. Leave them in the syrup for 20 minutes. Sieve the flour and add the sugar, the egg yolks, water and the stiffly whisked egg whites. Lift the potatoes from the syrup and coat them with the batter. Fry them in hot oil until crisp and brown. Drain them on soft paper and top them up with icing sugar and a lemon cut into a butterfly pattern.

Vegetables Dishes

Arrowroots with Beans in Coconut

Bean Egg Bhajias (Ankara)

Brinjals Cheese Meal

Brinjals with Cheese

Carrot and Leek Soup

Carrot and Celery Soup

Cassava Scoth Eggs

Cauliflower Pilau

Cheese Soup

Vegetable and Cheese Salad

French Dressing

Leek and Cheese Flan

Coconut Chutney

Coconut Fritters

Cream of Celery Soup

Cucumber Sandwiches

Eggplant and Egg Curry

Eggplant and Pumpkin Stew

Corn in Coconut

Potato and Eggs Curry

Egg stew

Eggs and Cheese Meal

Bean and Eggs Pie

Fried Sukuma Wiki

Fried Brinjals with Ugali

Hot Curried Eggs

Irio

Kachumbari

Kimanga (Beans and Cassava Mash)

Matoke in Coconut

Mbaazi za Nazi (Pigeon Peas in Coconut)

Brinjals with Macaroni

Mseto (Greengrams with rice)

Njahi

Peas and Eggs Curry

Okra with Tomatoes

Onion Soup

Pawpaw Stew

Pea Pilau

Cowpeas Stew (Borohowa la kunde)

Potato Salad

Potato Delights

Potato Tea Scones

Potato Pancakes

Salad Platter with Mayonnaise

Mayonnaise

Savoury Potato Pancakes

Spinach Soup

Stuffed Eggs

Tomato and Celery Soup

Tomato Suprises

Tomato Sauce

Tomato Juice Cocktail

Vegetables with Eggs

Vegetables with Groundnuts

Vegetables Cheese Pie

Vegetable Stew

Arrowroots with Beans in Coconut

½ kg arrowroots

½ c dried butter beans

2 sliced tomatoes

2 tsp curry powder

Salt

2 cups thin coconut milk

1 cup thick coconut milk

Method:

Soak the butter beans overnight. Cook them until ready. Peel and slice the arrowroots and arrange them in a pan, alternating with layers of beans and sliced tomatoes. Add curry powder and salt and pour in the thin coconut milk. Cook covered until soft and most of the liquid is absorbed. Either boil the thick coconut milk separately and pour it on the cooked arrowroot pieces or add it to the cooking arrowroot and boil until soft.

Bean-Egg Bhajias (Ankara)

2 cups of beans

1 tsp salt

A pinch of pepper

1 onion

2 eggs

A little water

Oil for frying

Method:

Soak the beans overnight and peel off the skins. Grind them into a paste with all the ingredients, except the oil. Heat the oil and fry spoonfuls of the mixture until cooked and brown.

Serve with tea, cornflour porridge or any other drink. You may eat them with dania and chillies if you wish.

Brinjals Cheese Meal

2 medium sized brinjals

1 or 2 beaten eggs

½ cup milk

1 tsp salt

Dry breadcrumbs

100g fat for frying

150g grated cheese

½ cup tomato sauce

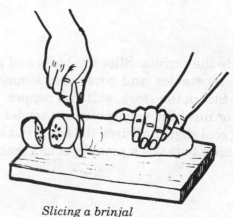

Slicing a brinjal

Method:

Wash and slice the brinjals in $\frac{1}{2}$ inch thickness. Mix the egg with milk and salt. Dip the brinjals first in the mixture and then in the breadcrumbs. Fry in hot fat until brown. Arrange alternative layers of brinjals, cheese and tomato sauce in a $2\frac{1}{2}$ pt casserole. Top with cheese. Bake at 350°F for 20 to 30 minutes. Serve immediately.

Brinjals with Cheese

3 medium sized brinjals	4 onions
Salt, pepper	5 tomatoes
25g flour	100 g grated cheese
$\frac{1}{2}$ c margarine	Parsley

Method:

Clean and wipe the brinjals. Cut into thin slices. Sprinkle with salt and keep aside. Blend the flour with seasoning, wipe the brinjals and toss them into the flour. Heat half the margarine and fry the brinjals until they change colour. Remove them from the oil and keep aside. Fry the slices of onion for a while and remove them from the fire. Place layers of brinjals, tomato slices and onions in a casserole, sprinkling them with cheese and seasoning. Cover the casserole and cook for 1 hour at 35°F. Remove the lid and sprinkle more cheese. Let the cheese melt. Serve garnished with chopped parsley.

Carrot and Leek Soup

$\frac{1}{4}$ kg carrots	1 lt chicken stock or water
$\frac{1}{4}$ kg leeks	Salt and pepper
2 large potatoes	A little milk
50g butter	

Method:

Peel and grate the carrots. Slice the leeks and peel and cube the potatoes. Melt the fat, add the vegetables and cover and simmer for 5 minutes, shaking the pan occasionally. Stir in the stock, salt and pepper. Bring to the boil. Simmer gently for 30 minutes, or until the vegetables are tender, stirring occasionally. Remove from the heat and cool slightly. Puree the soup. Put it back on the fire in a clean pan and add enough milk to make a pouring consistency. Heat it again on a low fire. Serve immediately.

Carrots and Celery Soup

1 large onion

$\frac{1}{2}$ kg carrots

4 stalks celery

25 g margarine

$1\frac{1}{2}$ litre stock or water

Salt, pepper

Pureeing the soup

Method:

Heat the fat and fry the chopped onion and diced celery until soft. Add the carrots and continue cooking for 5 minutes. Stir in the stock and seasoning. Simmer for 20 to 30 minutes, or until the carrots are cooked. Cool slightly and puree until smooth. Heat it again and serve with bread.

Cassava Scotch Eggs

$1\frac{1}{2}$ c boiled and mashed cassava

4 hard boiled eggs

1 raw egg

Dry breadcrumbs or minced groundnuts

Salt and paper

Oil for frying

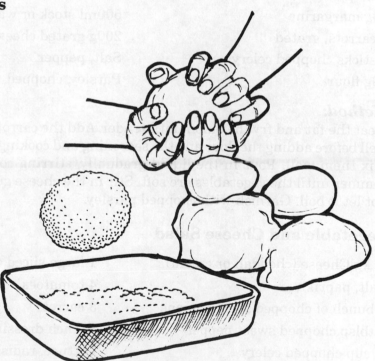

Covering the eggs in cassava

Method:

Mix the mashed cassava with seasoning. Divide it into portions and cover the boiled eggs with it. Beat the egg, dip in the cassava egg balls in it before dipping them into breadcrumbs. Fry in deep oil until golden brown in colour.

115

Cauliflower Pilau

2 cups rice	5 cloves
1 small cauliflower	1 piece cinnamon
1 cup peas	1 tblsp cumin seeds
2 large onions	4 tblsp oil
3 cardamons	4 cups water
Salt and pepper	

Method:

Wash and soak the rice. Cut the cauliflower into big pieces. Slice the onions finely. Heat the oil and fry the cardamon, cumin seeds, cinnamon and cloves, then the onions until light brown.

Add the cauliflower, peas, salt and rice. Toss them well, salt, pepper pour in the water and let it boil. Simmer until cooked and the water is absorbed.

Cheese Soup

1 chopped onion	500ml milk
50g margarine	500ml stock or water
3 carrots, grated	200g grated cheese
2 sticks chopped celery	Salt, pepper
50g flour	Parsley, chopped

Method:

Heat the fat and fry the onion until tender. Add the carrots and the celery and toss well before adding the flour and the seasoning and cooking slowly for a few minutes. Mix them well. Pour in the liquid gradually, stirring continuously until it boils. Simmer until the vegetables are soft. Stir in the cheese gently until it melts but do not let it boil. Garnish with chopped parsley.

Vegetable and Cheese Salad

$\frac{1}{2}$ kg Cheese (cheddah or cream)	1 large sliced onion
Salt, paprika	4 tomatoes
1 bunch of chopped spring onions	3 carrots
2 tblsp chopped sweet pepper	French dressing
$\frac{1}{2}$ cup chopped celery	Lettuce, radish for garnishing
1 cucumber	Mayonnaise

Method:

Mix the cheese, salt, paprika, spring onions, peppers, celery and a little mayonnaise. Chill them in a bowl. Turn out onto a large plate and surround with lettuce, slices of cucumber, sliced onion, grated carrots, tomato wedges and radish. Serve with French dressing.

French Dressing

A pinch of mustard	2. tbl. Vinegar
A pinch of black pepper	1 tsp sugar
Salt	1 C. oil

Put all the ingredients in a bottle and shake well.

Leak and Cheese Flan

150g savoury shortcrust pastry	125ml milk
2 leeks	2 egg yolks
50g cheddar cheese	Salt, pepper

Method:

Make the pastry and line a 7" diameter flan ring. Prick the base and chill.

Cut off the tops and roots of leeks. Slice and cook them in boiling salted water until tender. Grate the cheese. Mix the egg yolks with milk, cheese, salt and pepper. Sprinkle the leeks on the base of flan case, pour the custard mixture on them and bake for 30 minutes at 375°F.

Coconut Chutney

$\frac{1}{2}$ grated coconut	$\frac{1}{2}$ small bunch of dania (chopped)
Juice of 1 lemon	1 small onion (grated)
1 chopped chilli	Salt
4 pcs crushed garlic	A little water

Method:

Mix all the ingredients together. You can also use a blender to blend all the ingredients together for a few minutes. Serve with Bhajias

Corn Fritters

1 cup cooked corn	Salt, pepper
2 eggs	2 tblsp green pepper
$\frac{1}{2}$ cup flour	Oil for frying
$\frac{1}{2}$ tsp baking powder	

Method:

Sift the flour, salt, pepper and baking powder into a bowl. Beat in the corn, pepper and eggs until smooth. Heat the oil and fry spoonfuls of the mixture until cooked and browned. Drain and serve.

Cream of Celery Soup

1 medium head of celery	125ml milk
750ml stock or water	Salt, pepper
1 tblsp flour	125mls cream or evaporated milk
2 tblsp butter	

Method:

Clean and chop the celery finely. Simmer it in the stock until tender. Heat the fat and stir in the flour. Add the milk gradually and cook until it thickens.

Mix the celery and the flour mixture very slowly until well blended. Put them back on the fire and add the cream and seasoning. Garnish with parsley or cayenne pepper.

Cucumber Sandwiches

1 Loaf of bread	Salt, pepper
Softened butter	4 tomatoes
1 cucumber, peeled and sliced	Lettuce
2 tblsp chopped spring onions	

Method:

Slice the bread and spread it with butter. Arrange pieces of cucumber on one slice, sprinkle with onion, salt and pepper and cover with another slice of bread. Cut into neat pieces and serve garnished with lettuce and tomatoes.

Eggplant and Egg Curry

1 tblsp oil	$\frac{1}{2}$ c chopped tomatoes
2 onions, sliced	Salt, pepper
$\frac{1}{2}$ tsp garlic	1 large eggplant
$\frac{1}{2}$ tsp ginger	2 eggs
$\frac{1}{2}$ tsp curry powder	$\frac{1}{2}$ c water

Method:

Heat the oil and fry the onions, garlic and ginger until light brown. Add the curry powder, tomatoes, salt, pepper and chopped eggplant. Cover and simmer until soft. Stir in the beaten eggs until they set. Pour in the water and simmer until it thickens. Serve with rice.

Eggplant and Pumpkin Stew

$\frac{1}{2}$ kg eggplant (Brinjals)

2 large sweet peppers (sliced)

Salt

3 tblsp fat

1 chopped onion

$\frac{1}{2}$ kg minced meat (optional)

2 chopped tomatoes

$\frac{1}{2}$ kg cubed pumpkin

$\frac{1}{2}$ c water

Method:

Slice the egg plant and the pepper. Sprinkle the eggplant with salt. Heat the fat and fry the onion and meat until brown in colour. Add the tomatoes, peppers, pumpkin and eggplant. Season and pour in a little water. Cook until the vegetables are done. Serve on rice and garnish with parsley.

Corn in Coconut

2 green chillies

1 tsp cumin seeds

1 tsp corriander

5-6 peppercorns

$\frac{1}{2}$ tsp tumeric powder

2 tblsp ghee or fat

$\frac{1}{4}$ kg tomatoes

2 c coconut milk

$1\frac{1}{2}$ c boiled corn

Salt

1 bunch of dania

Pounding the spices together

Method:

Pound all the spices together. Heat the ghee and fry the paste and corn for 5 minutes. Add the tomatoes and cook until soft. Pour in the coconut milk and cook until it thickens. Serve garnished with dania.

119

Potato and Eggs Curry

$1\frac{1}{2}$ c oil

4 large sliced onions

3 cloves of garlic

1 tsp curry powder

3 tblsp dania

1 tsp tumeric powder

2 hard boiled eggs

1 kg potatoes, boiled in skin

Salt, pepper

$\frac{1}{2}$ c water

Method:

Heat the oil and sauté the onions. Add the garlic, curry powder, dania and tumeric and cook for a while. Blend in the eggs cut into halves and potatoes cut into four pieces. Add a little water and seasoning. Simmer for 15 minutes. Serve with chapatis or sliced bread.

Egg Stew

4 tblsp ghee or fat

2 sliced onion

1 tsp crushed ginger

3 cloves of garlic (crushed)

2 chillies

1 tsp cumin seeds

1 stick cinnamon

5 tblsp vinegar

$\frac{3}{4}$ c water

Salt

$\frac{1}{2}$ tsp garam masala

4 - 6 Hard boiled eggs

Method:

Heat the fat and fry the onions until golden brown in colour. With a little vinegar, pound into a paste the ginger, garlic, chillies, cumin seed and cinnamon and stir into the onions. Add a little water, the remaining vinegar, salt and garam masala. Cut the eggs in half length-wise and gently immerse them into the gravy. Simmer until the gravy thickens. Serve with rice or bread.

Eggs and Cheese Meal

1 tblsp margarine

$1\frac{1}{2}$ tblsp flour

Salt, pepper, paprika

250ml milk

1 cup of soft breadcrumbs

6 hard boiled eggs

$\frac{1}{2}$ cup cooked vegetables

Extra margarine

Method:

Heat the margarine and stir in the flour and seasoning. Add the milk, a little at a time, stirring until thick and smooth. Place half the crumbs in a casserole and arrange a layer of sliced eggs, cheese, vegetables and sauce on them. Cover them with the remaining crumbs and dot them with the extra margarine. Bake at 375°F for 50 minutes.

Bean and Eggs Pie

2 large sliced onions
2 tblsp margarine
1 cup cooked beans
2 tblsp chopped dania

Seasoning:
300g shortcrust pastry
4 eggs
1 egg for brushing

Method:

Heat the fat and fry the onions until soft. Add the beans, dania, salt and pepper. Heat well and keep aside.

Roll out the pastry and line a pie plate with half of it. Fill it with the beans. Break the eggs and pour them over the beans. Cover with the remaining pastry. Beat the one egg and brush the top of the pastry. Cut airholes on the pastry lid. Bake at 400°F for 40 to 45minutes. Serve hot or cold.

Fried Sukuma Wiki

$\frac{1}{2}$ kg *sukuma wiki*

1 tblsp fat

1 onion

2 tomatoes

Salt

1 tsp curry powder

$\frac{1}{2}$ c water

Method:

Clean and chop the *sukuma wiki*. Heat the fat and fry the onions until soft. Add the tomatoes, curry powder and chopped *sukuma wiki*. Pour in a little water, cover and cook for 10 minutes.

Fried Brinjals with ugali

2-3 tblsp fat or ghee
2 onions
$\frac{1}{4}$ kg chopped tomatoes
1 tblsp tomato paste
Salt

1 tsp garlic
1 tsp curry powder
2 or 3 sliced brinjals (unpeeled)
$\frac{1}{2}$ c water

Method:

Heat the ghee and fry the onions until brown and the tomatoes until soft. Add the tomato paste, salt, garlic and curry powder and fry until cooked. Fry the brinjals, add a little water, cover and simmer until soft. Serve with ugali.

Hot Curried Eggs

2 chopped onions

1 tblsp fat

1 tsp curry powder

4 chopped tomatoes

8-10 hard boiled eggs

1 tblsp fat

1 tblsp plain flour

$\frac{1}{2}$ tsp curry powder

$\frac{1}{2}$ tsp chilli powder

$\frac{1}{2}$ lt milk

Salt

$\frac{1}{2}$ cup cheese or fresh breadcrumbs

Method:

Chop the onions and fry in hot fat until soft. Add the curry powder and the chopped tomatoes and cook until the tomatoes soften. Cut the eggs lengthwise, separate the yolks from the whites and place the yolks in the pan. Mix well and put the yolks back into the whites. Place the eggs in a casserole with the yolks underneath. Heat the fat and fry the flour, the curry powder and the chilli powder. Stir in the milk and the seasoning to make a smooth sauce. Pour it gently over the eggs. Top with grated cheese or breadcrumbs and bake at 375°F for 15 to 20 minutes. You can also place it under a hot grill until golden brown in colour.

Irio (Kenyan Dish)

2 kg potatoes

1 kg peas

1 cob of green maize

Tomatoes for garnishing

Salt

Method:

Boil the potatoes, peas and maize separately. Mash together the potatoes and peas and mix them with the maize. Serve garnished with slices of tomatoes, fried mutton and sukuma wiki.

Kachumbari

2 onions

4 tomatoes

Salt

Juice of 1 lemon

1 tblsp chopped dania

A few green chillies

Method:

Peel and slice the onions very thinly. Sprinkle them with salt and keep them aside for sometime. Slice the tomatoes thinly and mix with dania, lemon juice, salt and green chillies.

Gently squeeze the onions until soft. This helps in removing the bitterness from them. Rinse with clean water, squeeze out excess liquid and mix with the tomatoes.

Kimanga (Cassava Beans Mash)

2 kg cassava

½ kg dried beans

Salt

2c thin coconut milk

1c thick coconut milk

Method:

Cook the beans until soft. Peel and slice the cassava and put them into the beans. Sprinkle them with the salt and the thin coconut milk, cover them and continue cooking until the cassava softens and most of the liquids is absorbed. Mash with the thick coconut milk. Continue cooking on low heat, stirring constantly until the milk is absorbed. The mixture should be thick. Serve with any stew.

Matoke in Coconut

½ kg meat

Salt to taste

10 raw cooking bananas

1 large sliced onion

1 tsp tumeric powder

1 tsp crushed garlic

5 chopped tomatoes

2 green chillies

1 tsp ginger

3 cups thin coconut milk

1 cup thick coconut milk

1 lime

1 tblsp chopped dania

Method:

Cut the meat into cubes and cook with salt and water until the liquid dries out and the meat is tender. Keep it aside.

Peel and cut the bananas into small pieces, clean them and place them in a pan together with the onion, salt, tumeric, garlic, chopped tomatoes, chillies, ginger and light coconut milk. Cook until all the milk is absorbed and bananas are soft. Add the meat and the thick coconut milk and continue cooking until the food is thick and saucy. Sprinkle in the lime juice. Just before serving, add the dania and serve whilst hot.

Mbaazi za Nazi (Pigeon Peas in Coconut)

½ kg mbaazi (pigeon peas)

Water

1-2 coconuts

A few cardamons

1 onions

1 tsp tumeric powder

Salt

Tomatoes

Method:

Clean the peas and soak them overnight. Cook them in water until soft but not mashy. Slice the onion and arrange it in the middle of peas in the pan. Add the tumeric powder, salt, cardamons and tomatoes and enough thin coconut milk to just about cover the peas. Cook until almost all the liquid is absorbed. Boil the thick milk separately, stirring constantly until ready. Pour it over the cooked peas. Serve with mahamri or any other meal.

Brinjals with Macaroni

300g macaroni - cooked	1 c flour
2 large brinjals	Salt, pepper
1 c tomato sauce or juice	1 c oil
1 tblsp margarine	1 c grated cheese

Method:

Peel and slice the brinjals into thin slices, sprinkle them with salt and dip them in seasoned flour. Fry them in hot oil until light brown in colour. Cook the macaroni in salted water until soft. Drain and add the butter and some tomato sauce. Arrange a layer of brinjals in a casserole, then a layer of macaroni and grated cheese, ending with a layer of brinjals. Cover with more tomato sauce and sprinkle with cheese. Bake at 375°F for 15 to 20 minutes.

Mseto (Green Grams in Rice)

1½ cups rice	1 coconut
1 cup green gram	Water
Salt	

Method:

Clean the rice and green gram separately. Boil the green gram until soft and dry. Put in the rice and enough thin coconut milk and cook until the rice is almost ready. Add the seasoning and the thick coconut milk. Cover the pan and cook until the liquid dries out. Serve with any thick stew.

Njahi

½ kg njahi

1 kg peeled potatoes

2 cobs of green maize

4 ripe bananas

Salt

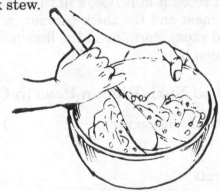

Mashing in the bananas

Method:

Boil the njahi and maize until cooked. Add the peeled potatoes and salt and boil until tender. Add the bananas and cook until ready. Drain off the liquid and mash them together. Serve with fried meat.

Peas and Eggs Curry

4 tblsp oil	Salt
6 hard boiled eggs	1 tsp tumeric powder
1 chopped onion	$\frac{1}{2}$ tsp cinnamon powder
2 cloves of garlic (crushed)	2 cloves
2 bay leaves	3 cardamon seeds
1 c chopped tomatoes	2 c water
2 chillies	$\frac{3}{4}$ kg shelled peas
1 tblsp chopped dania	Extra chopped dania
1 small piece of ginger (crushed)	

Method:

Heat the oil and fry the eggs until golden brown in colour and cut them lengthwise into halves. Put them aside. Fry the onions, garlic and bay leaf. Add the tomatoes, chillies dania, ginger, salt, tumeric, seasoning, cinnamon, cloves and cardamon. Pour in a little water and continue frying for a few minutes. Add peas and about $1\frac{1}{2}$ cups of water. Simmer until the peas are cooked. Gently add the eggs and cook uncovered for 5 minutes. Serve garnished with chopped dania.

Okra with Tomatoes

2 onions	A little lemon juice
10 okra	1 tsp ginger
3 chopped tomatoes	1 chilli
2 tblsp fat	Salt
$\frac{1}{2}$ tsp tumeric powder	Water
1 tsp cumin seeds	

Method:

Wash and chop the okra into pieces. Heat the fat and fry the onions until brown. Add the okra and cook until brown. Remove from the fat and keep aside. Add more fat, if necessary, and fry the cumin seeds, ginger, lemon juice, chilli and salt for a short time. Add tomatoes and water. Cook until it thickens and return the okra into the pan. Cook for a short while and serve garnished with dania. .

Onion soup

$\frac{1}{2}$ kg onions	Grated cheese
A little fat	Fried pieces of bread
1 litre of stock or water	Shallow oil for frying
Salt, Pepper	Parsley

125

Method:

Peel and slice the onions thinly. Fry them in hot fat until pale brown. Add the stock, salt and pepper. Simmer for 25 to 30 minutes. Pour the soup into a blender and puree it.

Fry the cubed pieces of bread in hot oil until brown. Pour the soup into a serving container and top with fried bread and grated cheese. Garnish with Parsley and serve immediately.

Pawpaw Stew

1 green pawpaw	3-4 pepper corns
3 tblsp fat	$\frac{1}{2}$ tsp tumeric
1 cup grated coconut	Salt
1 chilli	$\frac{1}{4}$ kg tomatoes
1 tsp ginger	2 cups water
1 tsp cummin seeds	

Method:

Grind the coconut, pepper corns, chilli, cumin seeds and ginger into a paste. Peel and cut the pawpaw into dices. Heat the fat, fry the paste until brown and add the tumeric and the pawpaw. Mix well, cook for 5 minutes before adding in the tomatoes, salt and enough water. Cover and cook until soft.

Pea Pilau

2 cups rice
1 cup peas
2 potatoes
2 onions
$\frac{1}{2}$ cup ghee
2 cloves crushed garlic
2 pieces cinnamon
$\frac{1}{2}$ tsp tumeric
4 cardamons
1 tsp jeera (cummin seeds)
Salt
Water

Pounding the spices together

Method:

Pick the rice and wash it. Shell the peas and peel the potatoes. Pound the cinnamon, cardamons and jeera together. Heat the fat and fry the onions until light brown. Add the spices and cook for a few minutes. Fry the rice until transparent. Stir well. Add the potatoes, peas and salt and continue frying for a while. Pour in 4 cups of water, cover and simmer until the rice is cooked. Serve with fried onions, fried potatoes and chopped hard boiled eggs.

Cowpeas Stew (Borohowa la Kunde)

1 cup dried beans	1 tsp curry powder
Salt	2 cups thin coconut milk
2 onions	1 cup thick coconut milk
A few cloves of garlic	1 chilli (optional)

Method:

Clean and soak the beans overnight. Cook them until soft, add the sliced onion, garlic, salt and curry powder. Continue cooking until the onions are soft and most of the liquid is absorbed. Mash together, pour in the thin coconut milk and cook until it thickens. Add the thick coconut milk and cook for another 5 to 10 minutes. Serve with chapati, rice or ugali.

Potato Salad

1 kg potatoes (cooked and diced)

$\frac{1}{2}$c mayonnaise

1 apple, peeled and chopped (optional)

Finely chopped onions

Chopped parsley

Chopping the onion finely

Method:

Combine all the ingredients with about 1 to 2 cups of mayonnaise. Serve on a plate and garnish with chopped parsley.

Potato Delights

200g cooked potatoes	50g margarine
300g flour	About 125ml milk
6 tsp baking powder	Jam or cheese for filling
$\frac{1}{2}$ tsp salt	

Method:

Cook and mash the potatoes and allow them to cool. Sift together the flour, baking powder and salt. Mix in the margarine in thin flakes and the potatoes. Knead with enough milk to make a soft dough. Roll out to $\frac{1}{4}$ inch thickness and cut out pieces with a large biscuit cutter. Fold the pieces into two and bake on greased baking trays for 15 minutes at 450°F. When cold, split them up and fill them with jam.

Potato Tea Scones

1 cup flour	1 tsp sugar
3 level tsp baking powder	1 cup mashed potatoes
1 tblsp margarine	About $\frac{1}{2}$ cup milk

Method:

Sift the flour and the baking powder and sprinkle in the sugar. Rub in the fat. Mix with the mashed potatoes and enough milk to form a soft dough. Roll to about $\frac{1}{2}$ inch thickness and cut out pieces with a scone cutter. Place on greased baking tray and bake at 400F for 12 to 15minutes. Cool and serve.

Potato Pancakes

6 small potatoes	*Seasoning:*
1 onion	$\frac{1}{2}$ tsp baking powder
2 eggs	1 tblsp oil
3 tblsp flour	2 tblsp milk
	Extra oil

Method:

Peel and grate the potatoes and keep them aside for a few minutes. Squeeze out the liquid and mix them with the eggs, grated onion and the rest of the ingredients to form a thick batter. Drop and spread the batter into a greased heated frying pan. Brown both sides over low heat. Drain and serve with sugar or apple sauce.

Salad Platter with Mayonnaise

1 lettuce	1c celery
2 carrots	$\frac{1}{2}$c nuts
1c peas	50g cheese
2 tomatoes	Mayonnaise
1 cucumber	

Method:

Clean and shred the lettuce. Scrap and cut the carrots into thin sticks. Boil and cool the peas. Slice the cucumber and dice the celery.

Arrange them neatly on a platter and serve with mayonnaise

Mayonnaise

1 egg

Salt

Pepper

Mustard

1 tblsp vinegar

1 tsp sugar

$1\frac{1}{2}$ c oil

Method:

Place all the ingredients, except the oil, in a blender. Blend them while adding in the oil gradually until the mixture become thick.

Savoury Potato Pancakes

250g potatoes

250g flour

1 grated onion

1 bunch dania (chopped)

A few green chillies

$\frac{1}{2}$ tsp salt

$\frac{1}{2}$ tsp crushed ginger

Fat for frying

Method:

Boil and mash the potatoes. Mix with flour and the rest of the ingredients, except the fat. Divide the mixture into small balls and roll them into thin pancakes on a floured board. Heat a little fat and fry both sides of each pancake.

Spinach Soup

25g butter

1 onion

$\frac{1}{4}$ kg potatoes

750ml chicken stock

$\frac{1}{4}$ kg spinach

Salt, pepper

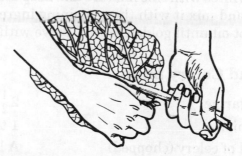

Pulling the spinach off the stalk

Method:

Melt the butter and fry the chopped onion until soft. Add the peeled and diced potatoes and toss well. Pour in the stock and simmer until the potatoes become tender. Wash the spinach and pull off the stalk and centre rib from the leaves. Add the spinach into the pan and boil for 10 minutes. Put the mixture in a blender and puree it. Return the blended soup into the pan, season well and reheat it before serving.

Stuffed Eggs

6 hard boiled eggs
1 green chilli

Filling:

$\frac{1}{4}$ tsp garam masala

1 tblsp dania

$\frac{1}{2}$ tsp gram flour

$\frac{1}{2}$ tblsp oil

$\frac{1}{2}$ tsp salt

Batter:

8 tblsp gram flour

8-10 tblsp water

$\frac{1}{2}$ tsp salt

1 green chilli

$\frac{1}{2}$ tsp ginger

Paprika powder

Oil for frying

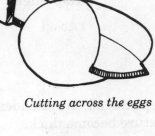

Cutting across the eggs

Spooning out the yolk

Filling the eggs with stuffing

Stuffed eggs

Method:

Cut across the eggs, remove the yolks and mix them with the rest of the ingredients. Fill the egg whites with this mixture and keep aside. Prepare the batter to a coating consistency and mix it with the remaining ingredients. Dip the eggs in the batter and fry in hot oil until golden brown. Serve with coconut chutney.

Tomato and Celery Soup

1 tblsp margarine

1 chopped onion

1 small head of celery (chopped)

$\frac{1}{2}$ kg skinned and chopped tomatoes

Salt, pepper

$2\frac{1}{2}$ pts stocks or water

1 tblsp flour

A little cream

Parsley for garnishing

1 tsp mixed herbs

Method:

Heat the margarine and fry the onions and celery until soft. Add the tomatoes, seasoning and herbs and cook for a while before adding the stock. Simmer until the vegetables are tender. Rub the soup through a sieve or liquidise in a blender. Thicken with a little flour if you wish to have a thick soup. Serve garnished with a little fresh cream poured into the centre and a sprig of parsley

Tomato Suprises

8 small tomatoes
50g grated cheese
Salt
Cayenne pepper

1 egg
25g seasoned flour
1 cup dry breadcrumbs
Oil for drying

Method:

Skin the tomatoes and remove the cores. Stuff them lightly with the grated cheese. Season well with salt and pepper. Roll them in flour, then in breadcrumbs. Fry in hot fat for 2 to 3 minutes until golden brown. Serve with salad.

Tomato Sauce

2 onions
50g butter
4 tblsp tomato paste

$1\frac{1}{2}$ cups water
Salt, pepper
2 tblspl vinegar

Method:

Fry the onions in hot butter. Add the tomato paste, water, vinegar, salt and pepper. Cook for 5 minutes and use as required.

Tomato Juice Cocktail

$\frac{1}{2}$ kg tomatoes
1 tsp salt
A pinch of pepper

1 tsp sugar
1 stick celery
2 tsp lemon juice

Method:

Place all the ingredients in a blender and blend for 30 seconds. Sieve with a fine holed sieve. Boil for a few minutes. Chill well and serve garnished in glasses.

Vegetables with Eggs

$\frac{1}{2}$c oil
1 green sweet pepper
1 red sweet pepper
2 onion
$\frac{1}{2}$ kg baby marrow

2 tomatoes
Salt, pepper
$\frac{1}{2}$c stock or water
2 beaten eggs

Method:

Heat the oil and fry the thinly sliced peppers, finely chopped onions, sliced baby marrow and chopped tomatoes. Cook for 30 minutes and add $\frac{1}{2}$ a cup of stock or water and the beaten eggs. Cook for another 3 minutes. Serve hot.

131

Vegetables with Groundnuts

2 bunches of green vegetables

1-2 cups water

3 tblsp pounded groundnuts

1 onion

1 tomato

Salt

A little oil

Method:

Remove the leaves from their stalks. Clean and cut them, if necessary. Heat the oil and fry the onion, tomato and vegetables. Add the groundnuts, seasoning and a little of water. Cook for 10 minutes.

Vegetable Cheese Pie

200g shortcrust pastry

100g grated cheese

1 cup milk

2 eggs

Salt, pepper

2 cups cooked vegetables

2 tomatoes

Method:

Use 50g of the cheese when making the pastry. Line a pie tin with the pastry and bake blind at 450°F for 10 minutes.

Mix the eggs, milk, seasoning and vegetables and fill into the pie shell. Slice the tomatoes and arrange them on top. Sprinkle with the remaining cheese. Bake at 350F for 30 minutes, or until cooked.

For shortcrust pastry, refer to recipe on an earlier page.

Vegetable Stew

2 tblsp fat

2 onions

$\frac{1}{2}$ kg diced potatoes

$\frac{1}{4}$ kg diced carrots

2 sweet sliced peppers

$\frac{1}{2}$ c chopped tomatoes

6 unripe bananas

2 tblsp tomato paste

1 tblsp chopped dania

1 tsp Paprika

Salt

750ml water

Method:

Heat the fat and fry sliced onions until transparent. Add the diced potatoes, carrots, green peppers, sliced tomatoes and bananas. Blend in the tomato paste, dania and paprika. Add the water and cook until the vegetables are tender. Serve with ugali.

Other dishes

Sweet Sima

Fried Rice

Tomato Rice

Spanish Rice

Plain Pilau

Rice (For Fish Pilau)

Hot Butter Sauce

Sweet Sima

3 c maizemeal flour
2 c boiling water
Enough sugar to taste
2 eggs
Oil for frying

Cooking maizemeal in water and sugar

Method:

Boil the water and sugar. Cook the maizemeal in this liquid to form a not-too-thick consistency. Shape into balls and coat with beaten eggs. Fry in hot oil until golden brown in colour.

Fried Rice

2 cups rice
$\frac{1}{2}$ cup fat
1 onion

Salt
$3\frac{1}{2}$ cups water

Method:

Heat the fat and fry the onion until soft. Add the rice and fry it for a few minutes. Add salt and water. Let it boil, cover and simmer until cooked.

Tomato Rice

1 kg tomatoes
1 tblsp margarine
Salt

1 cup water
$1\frac{1}{2}$ cups rice, washed
A little sugar

Method:

Combine all ingredients, except the rice. Place the rice in a greased casserole and pour the mixture over it. Cover and cook from the lower rack of the oven at 350°F for $1\frac{1}{2}$ hours.

Spanish Rice

1 onion
1 green pepper
25g butter
$\frac{1}{4}$ kg tomatoes
$\frac{1}{2}$ tsp salt

Pinch of sugar
1 bay leaf
150g rice
50g grated cheese

134

Method:

Melt the butter and add the sliced onion and chopped pepper. Cover and cook gently for 5 minutes, or until the vegetables are tender. Add the tomatoes, salt, sugar and bay leaf. Cover and cook for 15 minutes.

Boil the rice in salted water until soft. Drain it well. Add it to the tomato and onion mixture. Turn into a greased casserole and place in a hot oven at 350°F for 15 minutes. Serve sprinkled with cheese.

Plain Pilau

$\frac{1}{2}$ kg rice	1 tsp fresh ginger
2 large onions	1 c cooked peas
1 head of garlic	1 medium sized carrot
3 pieces cinnamon	2 tblsp Fat
6 cloves	3 c water
6 peppercorns	Salt
1 tblsp cumin seeds	

Method:

Pound all the spices together. Heat the fat and fry the onions until golden brown. Put spices, the carrot, peas and water. Salt and allow to boil. Add in the rice and cook until ready. Serve with beef stew or fish.

Rice (For Fish Pilau)

2 cup rice	1 tblsp cumin seeds
1 onion	3 sticks cinnamon
4 tblsp ghee	Salt
1 tsp tumeric	3 c coconut milk
1 tsp garlic	

Method:

Heat the ghee and fry the onion, cumin seeds and garlic until the onions become light brown in colour. Add the rice, tumeric and salt. Cook for a few more minutes. Pour in the coconut milk and let it boil. Reduce the heat, cover and continue cooking. Serve with fish.

Hot Butter Sauce

100 g margarine	4 tblsp cream
200 g sugar	1 tsp vanilla

Method:

Melt the fat. Blend in the sugar and the cream. Heat it but do not let the cream boil. Add the vanilla and serve.